RINDER'S RULES

RINDER'S RULES

Make the Law Work for You!

ROBERT RINDER

CENTURY

1 3 5 7 9 10 8 6 4 2

Century
20 Vauxhall Bridge Road
London SW1V 2SA

Century is part of the Penguin Random House
group of companies whose addresses can be found
at global.penguinrandomhouse.com

Penguin
Random House
UK

First published by Century in 2015

www.randomhouse.co.uk

A CIP catalogue record for this book is available from the British Library

ISBN 9781780894461

Typeset in Electra LH by Palimpsest Book Production Ltd, Falkirk, Stirlingshire

Printed and bound in Great Britain by Clays Ltd, St Ives plc

Penguin Random House is committed to a sustainable future
for our business, our readers and our planet. This book is
made from Forest Stewardship Council® certified paper

For Seth and for Marjorie

CONTENTS

INTRODUCTION

This book is not for morons. If you are one put it down at once. How will I know if I'm a moron? I hear you ask. Happily, there is a straightforward test. . . Last year I was asked to rule on a case in which a man, who had been given a tattoo gun for his birthday, had entered into an agreement with his friend. The agreement these two reached (after 10 pints of lager) was that they would both practise their artistic skills on each other. The birthday boy would start by tattooing a penis on his leg and, once his work was done, the gun would be handed over to his friend who agreed to do the same on his leg. The first man sat down and duly did as he had promised. His sense of proportion was affected by the amount of alcohol he had consumed and the result was a tattoo which went halfway down his leg (I was shown the photos). Upon seeing the outcome, this man's friend refused to keep his side of the bargain. He had sobered up by then. The first man then sued his friend for breach of contract, seeking the cost of removing the fifteen-inch penis tattoo from his leg. Now, here is the test. Answer the following questions:

1. Are you a person who thinks that purchasing a second-hand tattoo gun for a friend or loved one as a birthday present is a good idea?

2. Do you think that the first man has a reasonable legal case against his friend?

3. Would you have awarded any compensation to the first man?

If you have answered 'yes' to any of these questions then you are a moron. Goodbye!

For those of you still with me, you only need to know this: anybody (yes, that means you) can understand basic legal principles. Without any doubt you will have thought about the law at some point in your life. In fact, we think about the law all the time – every single day – and in countless different situations. Sadly, very often (too often) when something goes horribly wrong people do nothing or let an offending party get away with it because the law seems just a bit too complicated, or, worse still, people approach contentious situations in a manner which makes things far worse.

I have written this book for two reasons. Firstly, to empower you. Read on and you will know exactly what to do when confronted by a thorny legal problem. Secondly, to make my contribution to the de-moronification of the world (yes, I know that's not technically a word). This is a critical global mission. Just imagine how marvellous the world would be if everybody had a copy. In fact, if you have any sense of social awareness, if you have ever recycled anything for example, then it is not enough only to buy one. You need to go out and purchase this book for everyone you know. The world needs you! I realise that this may be mildly expensive but you and your loved ones could quite literally save fortunes by following Rinder's Rules and, think of this: you could spare me (and judges everywhere) from having to deal with completely pointless cases and thereby free up courts everywhere to deal with really important matters. It is, in other words, a complete win–win situation.

There are legal libraries filled with tens of thousands of books on each of the topics I have written about here, many of which are so painfully dull that they should come with a clear warning that 'readers should not operate heavy machinery', but these coma-inducing works are mostly written by and for lawyers. This is different. This book is for anyone. I do not care in what order you read the chapters of this book or where you read it. Some people after all (mostly men, it has to be said) achieve their most intellectually inspired moments whilst sitting on the loo. Before you begin turning the pages however, remember this: the book does not deal with every single legal situation you might confront. I have focussed on the areas of law that I am most commonly asked about as a barrister and the cases that I am invited to rule upon in my television courtroom. These are the types of legal issues, therefore, that you are most likely to face.

In each chapter you will find extraordinary tales of legal disasters from the UK and the USA (where the principles courts apply are often identical). The point of these stories is that, by reading them, you may learn what not do. The good news is that you do not have to work this out by yourself. I will provide you with a very simple set of logical rules at the end of each chapter which, applied properly, could be thoroughly life-changing. By buying this book you have already demonstrated that you are someone with a profound capacity to think logic-ally, so learning my rules should be an absolute doddle.

As some readers will know, I spent most of my career as a

barrister dealing with very serious national and international criminal cases, so I get bags full of (usually dreadfully written) letters from a variety of twittering oddballs asking why, when I am a criminal barrister, I am ruling on civil disputes. The answer is that nearly all legal cases have a common theme. Most of them come down to who is telling the truth and whether the person bringing a case has the evidence to prove it. The good news (for me) is that I am skilled in the art of lie-detection. If you have seen the show, you will know that I have a heightened sense of smell when it comes to lies. In fact, if I were an X-Man (a movie my godchildren love), that would be my mutant special power. Not as cool or useful as walking through walls or having titanium claws perhaps, but pretty helpful in my courtroom.

I cannot promise that this book will give you any lie-detecting super powers, neither will reading it turn you into a lawyer. But following my rules will prevent anyone ever attempting to take legal advantage of you and your family, which is worth the cover price on its own.

Good luck and enjoy. Do not write to me to complain. If you feel you must, for goodness' sake check your spelling and grammar or your letter will go straight in the bin.

CHAPTER 1

CONSUMER RIP-OFFS

I perfectly understand why people apply to have their cases heard in my courtroom. They want fair and speedy justice and, more importantly, they want the party they are suing to be in the full judgemental glare of millions. The overwhelming majority of those who apply to the show are those who have been ripped off by mega-companies and want me to help. It has become a common threat made by disgruntled consumers throughout the UK to put-upon staff representing British companies in call centres that, unless the matter is resolved, 'I'll take you on *Judge Rinder!*' Sadly, these threats are simply ignored as (surprise! surprise!) big companies refuse to have their cases heard in public. Given the letters I receive from people who have been ripped off (very often by large corporations), I would love nothing more than to meet at least one senior managing director who was brave enough to appear before me. Until that happens, I want to empower you, the consumer, by providing you with the legal tools you need to take on businesses yourself.

In this chapter you will read some truly horrifying tales of consumer rip-offs and learn what to do if and when things go wrong. If you follow my rules you should be able to avoid

---

legal trouble. If not, you will know exactly what to say to get your case resolved before it gets ugly. These next few pages could save you a fortune, so DON'T BE A MORON. READ THEM!

MOBILE PHONES

Thousands of people call ITV wanting to sue their mobile-phone company in my court. It is by far and away the most common consumer complaint I hear about. These multi-billion-pound companies are very often as pleasant at responding to consumer issues as a fart in a lift but, if you act carefully and know your rights, there is plenty you can do to avoid being taken for a ride.

Celina's story

Celina Aarons was a caring and considerate young woman. She lived a modest life within her means and looked out for her two siblings. In fact, she looked out for them so much that she committed the one mortal consumer sin we all know only leads to bad places: she agreed to pay her younger brother's mobile-phone bill. Just to be clear, anyone who does this without having absolute confidence that they can pay the bill in the event that the user cannot is a total fool! *Never, ever do this!* I promise you I won't be kind about your decision to be generous if you end up in my court! If a person can't afford to pay for a mobile contract then – in my view – they shouldn't have a phone!

Now, anyone who has signed their teenager up to a family plan with a big phone company because someone in a call centre convinced them that it would save them time and money will probably know what's coming. But Celina had more of a reason to support her sibling's phone habits: he was born deaf and unable to speak. Close to his sister but unable to call her if he needed her support, Celina's brother Shamir would text her instead. While he studied at college, Celina believed it was best that she covered Shamir's usually modest mobile costs, which tended to reach a maximum of $175. So imagine her surprise when, one day, she opened a monthly bill of $201,000.

Surely, Celina supposed, this must be some sort of ridiculous error. But a tearful conversation with the phone company later confirmed her worst fears: the payment really was due, and it was due soon. Shamir had crossed the border into another country, during which time he kept up his usual habits of texting and using the internet. Over two weeks his data roaming charges had gone through the roof, with T-Mobile charging $10 per megabyte. To put that in perspective, watching one video on YouTube for half an hour over your phone in your own country usually uses up 250 megabytes.

Needless to say, Celina was devastated. Her brother and his phone company had left her with a bill that could have paid for a house – all because of an ill-thought-out holiday. 'I asked, three, four times, are you serious?' she told WSVN-Channel 7 News. 'I was freaking out. I was crying, shaking. I was thinking, My life is over.'

Even though the phone company had apparently texted Shamir's phone four times over the period, warning that he was going over his data plan, nobody had informed Celina as the bill-payer. And even if they had contacted her to let her know that roaming charges were being applied, it was unlikely that she would ever have thought a phone bill could climb that high. Unable to pay the bill, she went to the media – and, possibly wanting to avoid bad press, T-Mobile eventually backed down and reduced her costs to $2,500. They also gave her six months to pay, rather than demanding it as one of her monthly bills.

Lessons from Neil

A little closer to home, one man in Sussex was fighting his own battle with Vodafone at the same time over an £800 bill he'd incurred after going on his own holiday. Neil Winton, a website publisher and freelance journalist, had gone on a jaunt to the US for two weeks and thought little of it, until he was slapped with a fee of £550.55 for January and £238.39 for February from the telecoms company. The phone company had sent Neil notices about roaming charges but they meant little to him. He had just purchased a smartphone for the first time – which just shows that the dangers of smartphone use go way further than Facebook-stalking your ex to the point of fatal embarrassment.

It was good news for Neil in the end though, as he went to the media to expose the company about its excessive charges and scared Vodafone silly. As attention escalated, they offered to reduce his bill by 25 per cent, then 50 per cent, and when he refused the final offer on principle and threatened to take them to the small claims court, they evidently decided it wasn't worth the bother and agreed to wipe all his charges. Corporations (a bit like school bullies), it turns out, are always the same: when push comes to shove, they're the biggest cowards of them all.

THE VERDICT

Being as fair as possible to the mobile-phone companies, Celina and Neil were to some extent the architects of their own misfortunes. Both signed contracts without reading and under-standing their content, something perhaps many of us have done.

A contract is a pretty simple legal concept made difficult by lawyers who have a vested interest in complicating things. It is a written or spoken agreement, especially one concerning sales, employment or a tenancy, that is intended to be enforceable by law. Celina and Neil may not have realised that they were entering into a contract, but this is what they did. By signing that they had read and agreed to abide by the mobile-phone provider's terms and conditions (T&Cs), they were verifying that they were satisfied to continue receiving the service on that basis.

Do I hear you shouting, 'But who reads the small print? It's not fair! It is written by lawyers, to protect companies and is totally impossible to understand!' You would be totally correct: however, sadly, that's life! It is your responsibility to read the terms and conditions and very much in your interests to do so. The law in many instances actually allows you a cooling-off period of 14 days to give you time to reflect and certainly to read the T&Cs if you have not already done so.

If you don't understand a term in the T&Cs then jolly well ask the company. If they can't reasonably explain it then it is probably not an enforceable term in any event. A contract has to be plainly understood by the company and by you. SO READ THE DAMN THING!

SO WHAT CAN I DO?

Lucky for the consumer, some legal changes have been made in the last few years that protect mobile-phone users from certain unseen charges. In 2014 the EU introduced new caps on how much a person on holiday could be charged for using their data.

And there's more good news: at the end of 2015 roaming charges in Europe are set to disappear completely. However, maybe you should do some soul-searching if you really are spending your expensive holiday browsing Wikipedia articles about the obscure ailment you're suddenly 90 per cent sure you've been suffering from for years ('But do you think this looks like a tapeworm infection or not, Bradley?' is something nobody wants to hear emanating from the en-suite bathroom), or, indeed, filtering out the cellulite from your bikini shots while 'relaxing' on the beach. Remember, boys and girls: the internet can be a dark place. *Check yourself before you wreck yourself.*

But what if it really does seem like your phone company has you in a bind, and you have accidentally ballsed up on a holiday outside the EU? Is all really lost?

- Receiving such an unexpected bill can be terrifying. There are some who could shrug the nasty experience off, pay the charge immediately and put it down to life, but those people are few and far between. When the tears have subsided and the tissue box is empty you have to think rationally. Hiding the bill in the back of a drawer and hoping it will go away on its own is a definite no-no.

- It may be shutting the gate after the horse has bolted, but now is a good time to find your copy of the terms and conditions and read them. If you have thrown them away (silly billy, you won't do that again) or can't find them, contact your telephone service provider by phone or internet, or at the shop you purchased the service from, and request a copy.

- Read your bill and ensure you understand what you are being charged for. Check whether it is for roaming charges, premium services, sending images, downloading internet data, phone calls, text or administration charges. It is of course possible that the service provider could have made a mistake. Check whether the charges they are imposing are in fact within the T&Cs.

- If you do not understand the charges speak with a friend or family member that you feel may have better comprehension of the bill; then contact the service provider and ask for the bill to be explained. Do not take your frustration and anger out on the person you are speaking to. They will invariably be more polite and willing to help if they understand you are not attacking them personally, but genuinely want to know how the charges are made up. Also they are very likely to be on a zero-hours contract somewhere in Mumbai! *It isn't their fault.* . . Wishing their sudden and excruciating death will not help matters.

- Write down what was said during the phone call. *This is an absolute must.* Memory at the best of times can let us down, even more so in stressful situations and when explanations are given in language that contains alien words such as 'roaming', 'megabytes', 'data download' etc. If you do not understand, do not be frightened to ask for explanations to be repeated. Above all, always obtain the name of the person at the company you were speaking to and record the date and time of the call.

- If you believe, or even just hope, the company have made a mistake, contact them and ask them to check the bill. If there was a mistake and they acknowledge it, ask them to confirm in writing their admission of error. You can then rest easy and make a promise to yourself to read all T&Cs in the future.

- If, however, you believe the bill is unjustifiably excessive and wrong or that the providers have acted outside their terms and conditions, contact them and politely point this out. Remember that if they have acted within the T&Cs that you signed up to, they are under no obligation to waive all or any of their charge. The ruder you are the less likely you are to get them to bend over backwards to help you.

- Legally there is very little, if any, wiggle room to avoid payment of any expenses you have incurred that were explained in the contract. Technically you may be able to challenge a contract if the T&Cs are written in such a lengthy, jargonistic, gobbledygookish manner that Joe Public would not be able to understand them, but generally the companies' highly paid legal advisers are aware of possible challenges and have constructed their contracts so that a court would consider them to be in language that anyone aged 18 or over, with no legal training, should understand.

- Very often companies will respond to customers' honest appeals explaining context and circumstances by reducing bills and agreeing extended repayment plans. Such offers should not be accepted initially but considered. It may be worth returning with further pleadings (be honest about what this has done to you emotionally) as this has been successful for some. However, be mindful that the companies are themselves often obliged to pay fees to providers in the host countries and almost certainly this aspect of the bill will not be negotiable.

- If agreement cannot be reached you should then contact an impartial free Alternative Dispute Resolution scheme (ADR), providing them with copies of your T&Cs, bills, any correspondence, and details of contact with the providers.

- Generally there are two ADRs used by the telephone companies: CISAS (Communications and Internet Services Adjudication Scheme) and Ombudsman Services Communications. You can establish from the Ofcom (independent regulator and competition authority for the UK communications industry) website which of the two ADRs the telephone service provider uses.

- The ADRs act as independent middlemen between the customer and telephone service providers. Decisions they arrive at are binding on the service providers and enforceable in law. If the phone company is found to be in the wrong it could be required to make an apology, correct the problem, and even pay an extra financial reward.

- There is nothing more you can do but learn for the future.

RINDER'S RULES

- Read the T&Cs and identify what and how charges will be incurred when you take out a phone contract. Tariffs between companies vary significantly. Speak to your provider and get them to explain charges and how you can reduce them. Establish whether they provide a package of data roaming bundles, what this includes and how much it costs. Check what other telephone providers offer. The T&Cs contain other very important information including your liability to pay bills for usage if the handset is stolen and you have not reported it to the police and provider at the earliest opportunity.

- Conduct research to see if it will be cheaper to buy a SIM in the country you are visiting. It often is.

- Turn off your data roaming setting on your smartphone. If you do not know how to do this, your provider will tell you how, or there is very good information (including videos) on how to do this on the extremely helpful Ofcom website. If you do not turn the roaming setting off, your smartphone will automatically seek out internet connections and you may use data without knowing it.

- Ensure that you make best use of free Wi-Fi in cafes, restaurants, bars and hotels, but ensure roaming is switched off. Apps, some free, can be downloaded showing where these are wherever you are. Of course, download the apps before you go abroad or when already connected to Wi-Fi or you will be blaming me for your excessive data bill.

- Regularly monitor usage. You can download an app to do this from your provider or check your account online.

- Do not sign a contract on behalf of someone else. At the end of the day, breaches of the contract or bills incurred are down to you. Word of caution: just watch my courtroom to see how many people who signed phone contracts for best friends with bad credit histories were let down and lumbered with big bills and the threat of bailiffs.

- Make sure that, if you do sign a contract on behalf of someone such as your children, you have the ability to ensure they do not exceed what you are willing to pay for. This may be difficult but can be achieved by telling them how they might incur excessive charges. Most children are way more savvy than you think (even grunting teenagers) and will take on board what you have told them.

- You can also set up passwords before premium or international numbers can be accessed and before apps can be purchased. Word of caution: the chances are that your children will know more about settings on the phone than you ever will. Many also know passwords you regularly use. Do, do, do remember teenagers' golden rule: 'Parents are stuuuuupid.'

BUYING DODGY GOODS

How many times have you purchased something from a company which wasn't up to standard but you didn't have the time or energy to take on the company or – more commonly – you were nervous about losing your case in court? READ ON AND BE BRAVE!

Colin and the lump of clay

Colin Marsh was a generous man. The bakery owner and his hairdresser wife hadn't always had it easy over the years, pulling together money when they could and sometimes having to go without. Their two young daughters, Daisy and Maddie, hadn't always had the best Christmas presents or the most expensive trainers. But then one year came around when Colin was determined that his little girls were going to get a real Yuletide treat: he got himself down to Tesco and picked up a brand-new £470 iPad. Christmas was sorted.

Or it would have been, if fate hadn't decided to be a little bit cruel to poor Colin. Come Christmas Day, Daisy and Maddie ran excitedly downstairs, tore open their stockings and then came to the big present under the tree that they knew was particularly special. Grinning with anticipation at what Santa could possibly have brought them, they carefully unwrapped the seasonal paper and peaked inside at the box of an expensive Apple product they'd never thought they'd be able to own. There were cries of glee, inhaled gasps of disbelief.

'Look inside,' Colin urged them, the hours slaving away as the head of his two bakeries all year suddenly seeming worth it. He peered over his daughters' shoulders to get a first glimpse of their hard-earned gift, and came face to face with . . . a lump of clay.

A few of you whose parents were – to put it politely – practical jokers might imagine that this was just a bit of a tasteless joke on the part of Colin. One of my friends' fathers, for instance, once wrapped up a duvet set that had gone missing from her bedroom the month before, with a packet of Smarties thrown in as a consolation prize that really added insult to injury. However, Colin hadn't intended to give Daisy and Maddie an old piece of impacted earth for their Christmas present that year, and he certainly wasn't happy about it. He was going to go straight down to the Tesco store he'd purchased it from the very next day and sort this horrible error out once and for all.

Unfortunately, seasonal luck wasn't smiling down on Colin. Come Boxing Day, he went to give the store a piece of his mind for ruining Christmas Day for his little ones – and was told a refund wouldn't be possible until Tesco had completed a thorough investigation. A couple of hours later, the local police station called to ask him for an interview to get the ball rolling on tracking down whichever scammer had tampered with the iPad. It all seemed fairly understandable and routine. Little did our hero know, however, that Tesco had decided he was the most likely candidate – and as soon as he attended the police station he was locked in a cell on suspicion of fraud for over three hours. Merry Christmas!

Eventually, some serious action was taken and the iPad which should have been in the box that Maddie and Daisy opened the day before was tracked down to an address in Wales, 200 miles away – proving that sometimes, the Apple falls spectacularly far from the tree. Since the police were at least 50 per cent sure Colin wasn't able to teleport between addresses at lightning speed, they finally released him at the end of the day and made one of those 'sincere apologies' you always see cut and pasted into emails. The Marshes got their refund and, eventually, Daisy and Maddie got their iPad. But in my day we would have kept the old piece of clay. And we would have liked it.

THE VERDICT

In Colin's case he purchased a product that was well advertised, nationally and internationally, from a long-standing high-street trader. This wasn't a bottle of perfume purchased from a market stall which *quelle surprise* turns out to be coloured water. Although I am sure some people have taken possession of the occasional iPad with some problems, generally they are of satisfactory quality, as described, and fit for purpose. Colin's problem appears to be that before his children actually opened the iPad packaging on Christmas Day, someone had switched the contents, so that the weight was unlikely to arouse suspicion. Where this happened would be difficult to prove, but it is clear that it was not Colin who was responsible.

Now, I am not attempting here to give traders in general a kicking. They are very often the victims of crime and it would also be difficult for them to say whether a product was supplied to them having already been tampered with, whether their own staff tampered with it, stealing the iPad, or whether the theft of the item occurred after they supplied the customer.

What I am trying to point out is that sometimes things are not black and white. In Colin's case common sense just had to prevail. He was the victim. He was clearly hard-working and, with no evidence to the contrary, honest. Who could believe (well, Tesco and the police initially did) that a father could be so cruel to his children on Christmas Day?

So what can we learn from this? It would be too easy to say we should open the packaging of products when we buy them. This would really impress your in-laws, unwrapping an already-opened gift. Although this would be a solution, I can see some difficulties taking your new washing machine out of its box at the checkout, with the queue twenty deep behind you.

SO WHAT CAN I DO?

So what do you do if you find yourself in Colin's unenviable position? Whose fault is it if the product has been tampered with, and how can you prove that you didn't do it yourself? Are you entitled to a refund, and are you realistically likely to get it? And how common are these consumer frauds, especially around high-risk buying times like Christmas? Just last year a similarly bizarre occurrence reared its head in Washington when a teenage girl opened what she thought was a pair of Beats by Dre headphones from Wal-Mart and they turned out to actually be cleverly disguised packs of tuna fish.

The Sale of Goods Act

One of the few good things to come out of the seventies (a decade of little merit to speak of apart from my birth) was that

Parliament did something of use by giving consumers clear statutory rights for the first time.

- Consumers today have rights under the Sale of Goods Act 1979 which is an absolutely brilliant (and rather easy to read) piece of legislation. According to this Act of Parliament, a product must be of satisfactory quality, fit for purpose, and as it was described by the seller. If it isn't, you can get one of the following:
  - a repair
  - a replacement
  - your money back (a refund)
  - some of your money back

These rights do not apply if:

1. There is nothing wrong with the goods – you have just changed your mind about wanting them. 'My partner says that my bottom looks above averagely large in this!' is not a grounds for getting a refund (although I think in law it should be).
2. You examined the goods when you were buying them, and the fault you want to complain about was so obvious that you should have noticed it. If there was a hole at the bottom of bucket but you bought it anyway because it was a lovely shade of fuchsia, you can't complain when the shop that sold it to you tells you to get lost when you grumble that your floors are ruined!
3. The seller pointed out the defect that you now want to complain about. This is more tricky – sellers will often claim they told you about the problem. In

order for that to be any kind of defence, the seller has to have been incredibly precise about the defect.

4. You have damaged the goods yourself. You're a total fool if you don't understand that you can't get your money back for an item that you damaged!

5. The problem is the result of normal wear and tear. This is another one which companies (particularly car dealers) use to refuse to give you a refund. Most of the time they are talking absolute rubbish. It all depends on how long the thing you have bought can reasonably be expected to survive. This obviously varies from item to item and will depend on what a third-party expert says about how long the thing should last. You can usually find reliable information on this online these days for almost everything from clutches to carpets.

6. The goods have lasted for as long as could reasonably be expected. You can't sue for a coat which has fallen apart after 12 years of wearing it just because someone came up to you and gave you pocket change thinking you were homeless and offered to do a fun run on your behalf.

- If the goods you have bought are not of satisfactory quality, as described, or fit for purpose, you have the right to return the goods and get all your money back! (By the way, a full refund includes the cost of all postage and packing.)
  - ○ **'Satisfactory quality'** means minor and cosmetic defects as well as more serious problems.
  - ○ **'As described'** refers to any advert or verbal description made by the trader.

- **'Fit for purpose'** covers not only the obvious purpose of an item, but any purpose you queried and were given assurances about by the trader.

- The right to reject goods and get a full refund only lasts for a relatively short time, after which you are deemed to have 'accepted' the thing. How long a 'short time' is will depend on what the product is. This does not mean that you have no legal action against the seller after this time, just that you are not automatically entitled in law to a full refund.

- If it has been more than 12 or 28 days (depending on the T&Cs, which you have of course read), then normally the company has a duty to repair or replace the thing you have purchased.

- Just to be clear: the Sale of Goods Act also covers second-hand items and sales. But if you buy privately (including online), your only entitlement to your money back is if the goods aren't **'as described'**. You may often see second-hand items advertised as 'bought as seen', and this is often replicated on receipts. In effect it exonerates the seller from legal liability if the product does not work or ceases working two days later.

- Here's a good tip: in law, if goods which are expected to last six months do not (this is pretty much everything apart from food), it will be presumed that the goods did not conform to the contract at the time they were bought unless the seller can prove otherwise. In other words, it will be up to the seller to prove that the goods were in good working order and not you! In most other circumstances in UK law, it is up to you to prove that the thing you purchased was defective.

- Whatever you have bought, you only ever have six years from the time you bought the thing in which to make a claim, irrespective of how long the goods actually last.

RINDER'S RULES

- The bottom line is that it is usually sensible to purchase items from long-standing reputable companies, instead of from Big Dave down the market. Your purchase of perfume may end up smelling more of the English Channel than Chanel No.5.

- If you have purchased defective goods, basically (yes, I use that word which I normally tell people off for, but it is basic) all you can do is to bring the imperfect – or missing – item to the notice of the seller as soon as practicable. Do not handle an obviously subsituted product if possible as quite evidently a crime has been committed. The item, in Colin's case a lump of clay, may have yielded evidence. The police may be able to examine the item for DNA or fingerprints.

- If you do not receive satisfaction from the trader, retain the goods and if you paid for them with a credit card you should contact your bank or card company and inform them of the disputed transaction. You should then contact your local Trading Standards department who may be able to investigate your complaint.

- If all else fails and you are sure that you are in the right (you have gone through this chapter carefully and considered the circumstances of the situation against the Sale of Goods Act) then take the seller to the small claims court. There is a helpful section at the end of the book which tells you exactly how to do this.

ROTTEN FOOD

The internet is awash with tales, real and embellished, about fast-food jaunts gone wrong, chicken tumours found in nugget boxes, deadly spiders suddenly bursting free from imported packs of bananas and human thumbs floating in cans of cola. What are you supposed to do if you find a little unappetising extra in your food? Are you due more than a refund, especially if the whole ordeal causes you to experience mental and physical distress? Do you have to accept it if you're offered the equivalent of a waiter telling you 'Pipe down or everyone else will want one' when you complain about a fly in your soup or a reptile in your salad? And who is responsible, if the food in question is being sold in one shop but quite possibly delivered from another supplier altogether?

Robin's reptile

It's the second worst reptilian-related nightmare you could imagine befalling a big city, right after the return of Godzilla. Thirty-one-year-old Robin Sandusky was trying to take it easy and add some greens to her diet by buying a salad, in Manhattan

– when she ended up with way more than she bargained for. Chomping her way through a kale salad, in a remarkable stroke of luck she looked down, saw something a little different and thought, Oh, is that a bit of asparagus?

No such luck, Robin. In fact, what she'd very nearly just wrapped her lips around was a severed lizard's head. Take a deep breath and read that again. Makes Colin's experience with the clay iPad seem almost like good fortune, doesn't it?

Needless to say, kale-loving Robin quickly checked that severed reptile heads weren't part of the latest New York list of trendy health foods and, summarily reassured, made her way back down to the Guy & Gallard store to ask just what they were doing adding surprising extras to her salad. After all, mutilated animal parts in your lunch are supposed to be the domain of *I'm a Celebrity*. One doesn't attend a salad shop looking for mangled animal carcasses.

THE VERDICT

The store offered Ms Sandusky a replacement salad for her trouble – which, funnily enough, she declined. Instead, she walked away with a $4 refund and the knowledge for the rest of her life that she might have partly digested lizard eyes. Delicious.

SO WHAT CAN I DO?

- The food you buy from the supermarket, much the same as any other product, should be safe, of satisfactory quality, fit for purpose, and as described. (I'm sure Robin's salad wasn't labelled 'Special Offer: Extra Protein.') This isn't difficult! Food is unsafe or of poor quality if it is mouldy, has gone off, is out of date or is contaminated. If you find something that's not supposed to be there in your food, or if it's a little green around the edges and still in date, if you haven't eaten all of it try to preserve it as evidence (yes, I know, but it may be incredibly important – easier to keep a bit of the food before you've eaten it than to extract it after!). Put it in a sealed freezer bag or a Tupperware box and take it back to the store (within a reasonable amount of time – they can't tell if your sandwich had maggots in it if you have left it so long that more maggot friends have joined the party) and go to customer services.

- If you aren't satisfied with this, you can send a sample or a photograph to the manufacturer. If it was a Tesco salad (or M&S or Lidl – little critters don't discriminate in choice of supermarket), the manager at the store may do this for you, but if not you may have to send it to the manufacturer yourself along with a complaint letter. There is usually an address or a phone number 'if you are in any way unsatisfied with this product' on the packaging somewhere. You strictly don't need the receipt if the product is faulty, but if you have it, send a copy.

- They might not give you anything, but if you explain in your letter just how grossed out you were by finding Lizzy the lizard in your food and how you have been emotionally and physically affected by her appearance, they may offer you compensation, often in the form of vouchers. Don't expect this amount to be astronomical: despite what you may think, you won't be rolling in dough, but it could very well be worth the time and effort spent writing the letter. Stories about people getting millions from fast-food restaurant chains after finding something unpleasant in a burger are complete nonsense.

What about restaurants?

- When you eat out the law says that food that is served to you, just like food bought in a supermarket or products bought in a shop, should be safe, of satisfactory quality, and what it is described as (have I repeated myself enough yet?). The food should have come from a reputable source and should have been kept at the correct refrigerated temperature, prepared hygienically, and served at the correct temperature with clean utensils. If it is advertised as free-range chicken it should not be roadkill rabbit.

- Most restaurants are safe and fully compliant with hygiene regulations but if you are unsatisfied with your food because it is too cold, you have as much right to complain as if a cockroach was doing the breaststroke in your soup. I would suggest in the first instance, though, that you stop eating it.

- Depending on how extreme your grievance is – number one being too cold and number ten athletic insects – you have options. You can politely ask for a replacement meal or order something else. You can decide enough is enough and leave the restaurant. You should not have to pay for the rejected meal but you will have to pay for other food or drinks you have consumed. It is totally legal to refuse to pay because you believe the food was not of satisfactory quality; however, be prepared for discontent by the restaurant.

- The restaurant may be unhappy about your refusal to pay for your rejected meal; however, as long as you pay for whatever else you had, you can deduct the price of the rejected meal (and service charge, should you wish) and leave your name and contact details. If the restaurant calls the police, they will not get involved as it is a civil dispute. The restaurant can pursue you legally for the bill and in the worst-case scenario a small claims court can sort it out.

- Most people now carry a smartphone with a camera: take a picture of Charlie the cockroach and get your dining partner to seize and retain it (a serviette may suffice and the restaurant may even give you a takeaway container, but don't bank on it). If your chicken Kiev contains a lucky rabbit's paw, do the same. If there are witnesses at other tables, they may be willing to give you their names and contact numbers; after all, you may have saved them from a nasty experience.

- If there are issues of bad hygiene (or worse) you should contact your local food-standards department and environmental-health department. They will decide whether an investigation should take place and who will conduct it. Food-safety officers are responsible for enforcing food safety and standards rules in restaurants and takeaways.

- If you had no complaints about the food at the time but get food poisoning, and you are sure it is down to your meal, you may be entitled to compensation. You should see your GP, who will treat you. If the circumstances are appropriate, particularly if you are the third patient that day with food poisoning, all having visited the same restaurant, the doctor may notify the health authorities as urgent intervention would be necessary to ensure there are no further casualties.

- The doctor is likely to conduct analysis to establish what caused your illness and should be willing to support a claim for a refund from the restaurant for compensation, including the cost of the dish, pain or suffering, loss of earnings if you were off work, and any other expenses incurred as a direct result of the food poisoning. However, it may be difficult to prove whether it is the restaurant's fault. You would be best served by getting advice from a solicitor as soon as possible.

RINDER'S RULES

- British people tend to be incredibly conflict-averse in restaurants. Food is no different from any other consumer good in law. Do not accept poor quality. I don't care if the chef will be offended or if you are worried someone will spit in your soup (they won't, by the way!). Do not accept a substandard meal. If you bought a T-shirt which was ripped and damaged you would send it back. Food is no different! Demand exactly what you were promised.

- Always be polite but firm and remember you do not have to pay if you are unable to eat the food that has been dished up.

- If you have purchased food from a store, remember to keep evidence (including photos) of anything suspect.

- Return it to the shop and write immediately to the head of customer services AND the store manager demanding a refund and compensation.

- Do not expect to make millions just because you found a snail in your soda pop. You can only recover a limited amount of money when something like this happens (despite what you may have heard!).

PROVIDING POOR QUALITY SERVICES

The 1980s were a pretty splendid decade for the tasteless consumer. The government of the day, led by Mrs Thatcher of course, decided that even those who chose to purchase fluorescent high heels and matching shoulder-padded jackets deserved greater protection under the law, and so they passed the Supply of Goods and Services Act. This extended the law so that it not only applied to things you purchased but also to services you might use: everything from massages to make-up artists are covered by the legislation, and, in many cases, you are protected by other laws specific to the service you are using. I have included a holiday example here to illustrate exactly what to do when a service which was promised was a disaster; but – just to be absolutely clear – the law applies to anyone who is holding themselves out as providing a service of any kind whatsoever!

Patricia and George and their nightmare holiday

Patricia and George were the kind of sweet retired old couple you might pass by on the street and help with their shopping bags; the kind who might invite you inside for tea and biscuits, and tell you about the time they were courting; the kind who owned a beloved 13-year-old dog called Max, whom they walked along the same route every day, and were devastated when he passed away. They were looking for a peaceful break away from it all to grieve for Max and spend some time in the sunshine as a couple, to really reconnect and to enjoy some of their twilight years together. In other words, they were not the kind of people who you look at and think: 'By God, these two could really do with a rejuvenating 18–30s style getaway to Malia. Lads, lads, lads!'

Yet, confusingly, this is exactly what one travel agent decided when Patricia and George went in with the story about their lost dog and their desire to relax on a secluded beach away from it all. Promptly, the morons behind the counter at their local outlet booked them into a resort which boasted online reviews talking about all-night clubbing and copious vomit in the pool. Unless elderly Patricia was planning to drown her sadness in flaming absinthe shots and 70-year-old George was secretly planning to don a luminous Borat-style mankini and hit the beach with a couple of babes, this holiday was destined for painful failure.

Luckily, Patricia's daughter had the foresight to feel vaguely suspicious about Malia as an over-60s destination and research the hotel her mother had been offered. Once she'd read the reviews, she let the pair know in the politest possible terms that they probably would appreciate booking themselves into a resort where the free breakfast was more 'continental buffet' than 'routine chlamydia injection'. Pat and George rang up the agency, mentioned these concerns, and were assured that her daughter was probably right. They were transferred into a villa on another island less associated with upping the international teen pregnancy rates, and by all accounts had a lovely time.

The trouble started when they returned home to England, and it very quickly became a nightmare. The agency, it turned out, had charged the couple for both holidays. They claimed that Patricia and George had agreed over the phone to both charges, and said that they could listen themselves to recordings of the phone calls – but only if they paid £25 per recording. Despite the fact that P and G ended up taking them to the small claims court and winning the case, they still weren't paid – and payment was delayed again, even after a second case was brought before a judge. When they eventually, exhausted, went to the press with their story, they were told that it was merely an 'administrative error' that was preventing their refund.

THE VERDICT

In Patricia and George's case it seemed that going to the press served as a quiet reminder to the company to come good on their refund. The newspapers may not always want to run every disaster story, but suggesting that it's an option could work – alternatively, persevering with the claim can do the same trick.

SO WHAT CAN I DO?

So where exactly do you stand, if you buy a service that you are assured is 'perfect for you' and later realise that it doesn't meet your needs at all? Is there a legal precedent to protect older people from 18–30s holidays, and if so, would it work if you were a group of up-for-it *Geordie Shore* wannabes mistakenly sent to a Buddhist resort exploring the concepts of silence and modesty in the countryside?

- The good news is that in addition to the Supply of Goods and Services Act there are numerous laws which govern the duties and responsibilities of people supplying services. For example, the Consumer Protection from Unfair Trading Regulations provide you with protection from unfair or misleading trading practices; this includes misleading omissions and aggressive sales tactics. The regulations cover many types of sales, including holidays, vehicle servicing, replacement windows, insurance, car sales . . . in fact, practically anything you can think of.

- Companies are not allowed to use underhand tactics to get your business. So it is unlawful for a company to claim, for example, that they have a diamond ring (ordinarily worth £10,000) which they are selling for a fiver when in fact they only have one at that price – giving you almost no chance of getting it!

- Service providers (which includes travel agents and others) must never misrepresent (that's a lawyers' word for lying about something) the service or product they are selling. So informing you that you are booked into a five-star all-inclusive hotel in Palma, when you end up at the two-star Hotel Hell, a mere six miles outside the town centre, is an absolute no-no!

- Service providers cannot falsely state that their service will only be available for a very short time, or at a certain price for a limited time, to make you buy there and then. All that aggressive selling is a total breach of the regulations and you can sue for it! I told you that reading this book would be worth your while. And, yes, I am always right!

- The Regulations offer protection against service providers who are economical with the truth, or miss out key information that you might need to make your decision. So a travel agent who says the hotel is just a walk from the beach may not be lying, but it may be a four-mile walk, which you certainly never envisaged! Again, if this happens you are clearly entitled to compensation.

- It is considered 'misleading' if a service provider:
  1. Leaves out material information that the average consumer needs in order to make an informed decision to buy, or
  2. Hides or provides important information in an unclear, unintelligible, ambiguous or untimely manner. In other words, 50 pages of terms and conditions written

by Shyster Partners law firm in partial Latin simply will not do! If you cannot understand the terms and conditions, then there is a very good chance that the document you have received is unlawful. All legal documents should be capable of being understood by anyone who is able to read and eligible to vote. And yes, that means *you*!

RINDER'S RULES

- If the deal you are being offered looks too good to be true, that's because it is. Stay well away.

- Know your legal rights. They are not hard to understand. If you can read this book, you are more than intelligent enough to take on a dodgy company!

- Make sure you tell the service provider straight away that you are unsatisfied. Specify exactly what you want and demand an answer within 28 days.

- If you don't get a satisfactory reply, use the small claims court. It is easy to do, no lawyers are required, and this book can help you on your way. Just make sure you've read the whole thing and not just the amusing stories!

MY DELIVERY
HASN'T ARRIVED

Now, we don't often hear about this type of problem but it's still a recurring and very valid one. You've ordered something online, and paid for it, in exchange for a promise that the item/service/goods will be delivered to a chosen address, on time and in a perfect condition. However, sometimes the best placed orders don't make it to your door.

A *late delivery from Waitrose*

Finally, the saddest story of all: a woman who never got her Waitrose delivery. This tale of unending woe was considered so serious in March 2015 that the *Guardian*'s Money section dedicated an entire article to exploring what could possibly have gone wrong. After all, one day it's £90 worth of Waitrose food and the next it could be the entire country's dignity.

The woman, who chose to remain anonymous lest that notorious hard man John Lewis should track her down and strangle her with a strand of low-carb gluten-free tagliatelle, wrote in to the respectful left-wing newspaper to complain that she'd ordered everything for her Christmas dinner online and it had subsequently never arrived. Christmas had been ruined, and it was a mystery where the food had disappeared to, although the website seemed to claim that a delivery had been attempted at some point. By then it was so near to Christmas Day that Waitrose sent an automated message saying the food could no longer be brought to the house, and promised to issue an immediate refund.

Despite our anonymous woman's previously evangelical faith in Waitrose, she was shocked to find a couple of months later that she had in fact been charged for the food she'd never had the opportunity to enjoy. She emailed Waitrose – twice – and got no response. Eventually, the problem was solved by taking it to the *Guardian*, something we seem to hear again and again when companies won't get their legal bottoms in gear but are terrified of having their idiocy publicised, so back down in the face of newspaper power. Everyone had a little cry into their hand-knitted organic yoghurt friendship bracelets and then left the therapist's office and continued with their day of charity work.

SO WHAT CAN I DO?

In this case, a lot of Christmas deliveries from a number of different supermarkets had failed to get the turkey there on time, and the country was awash with disappointed people who never received their Whole Foods tofurkey or their frozen canapés from Aldi. So what do you do if you're in this situation and the shop won't even extend you the courtesy of a phone call? Do Waitrose owe you more than a refund if the roast potatoes aren't on the table come Christmas because of their cock-up? And does it matter if they may have attempted to deliver to you, but you weren't home or you weren't aware?

- Whether it is a Christmas hamper or a washing machine, the transaction is the same. You entered into a contract with the supplier to have the item delivered at a certain time. If the company fails to deliver when they said they would, you have legal rights.

- Firstly, you need to contact the courier, who may or may not also be the supplier, and find out what is happening. Contact details will usually be on your invoice but more often than not are repeated by the suppliers (particularly bigger stores) in an email. If they give a reasonable explanation, such as the delivery lorry being involved in a collision, or they quite honestly admit messing up and making a mistake, you may accept this, if there is a guarantee of next-day or other suitable time delivery, in which case it is nearly a happy outcome.

- However, 'tomorrow' (or, in the case above, 'after Christmas') may not be good enough. If you ordered by telephone or online (from an EU-based company) under the Consumer Contracts Regulations, you can cancel the order within 14 days and obtain a refund of the item's cost from the supplier. Delivery costs may be refunded because you specified the date and the company failed to honour its commitment, but there is no obligation on the company to refund those charges unless you paid an extra charge for a delivery on a certain date.

- If you placed an order at the store you are not afforded the same protection unless you had recorded on the invoice a date of delivery and the words 'time is of the essence'. This is important in contract law and you can legally cancel your contract if the delivery is not made on that date.

- If no date was specified the supplier must deliver within 30 days; you can then legally cancel the contract.

- If the item has not turned up, or the couriers left it in your dustbin at a time you were not in and not agreed by you, and it's gone missing, this is the responsibility of the suppliers and you should contact them.

- If you have taken extra time off work for the rescheduled delivery you can make a claim for compensation. You should correspond with the suppliers (using a service that provides proof of delivery) laying out your claim. It is more difficult, but you can claim for compensation if you can prove you have suffered substantial distress or inconvenience, and only having cornflakes and frozen fish fingers for your Christmas dinner may just fall into that category.

- As with all disputes, you should discuss the issues with the company before resorting to court action. Bigger companies are likely to have grievance or complaint procedures that will encompass non- or late delivery. If you are knowledgeable about your legal rights you are more likely to resolve the issue in a manner that is satisfactory to both of you. If they do not agree you have up to six years to enforce your claim at court.

- If you do have to go to court, and the value was up to £10,000, you should proceed in the small claims court. If the value was above £10,000, firstly, what kind of Christmas dinner were you planning?! and secondly, it will probably be best to seek legal advice for your claim, as you won't be in the small claims court and it all gets a bit more complicated. Remember, you don't have to go straight to a solicitor, your local Citizens Advice Bureau can help.

RINDER'S RULES

- Only order deliveries from reputable suppliers (check all reviews online before using an internet-only company).

- Make sure you specify the time and date of the delivery if ordering from a shop.

- In the event that things do not arrive on time, alert the company at once and specify a precise time you want the goods to be delivered.

- Read everything I have set out above – this will give you all the information you need and will prevent you from sounding like a clueless moron on the phone when you complain.

- For goodness' sake keep dated records of whom you spoke to and what was said from beginning to end.

CHAPTER 2

HOLIDAYS
FROM HELL

I receive bags of letters each week from people who have
had disastrous holidays and want to know what they can do
to get their money back. Those who write to me are very often
deeply distressed by their experiences. I completely understand why. We invest a huge amount of money and time in
organising and arranging our holidays; they are, for most
people, the one thing they genuinely look forward to in the
year (as opposed to pretending. . . 'Yes, dear, I can't wait to
see your mother for tea [*cough*]'!). As a result we all – perhaps
inevitably – ramp up our expectations. We assume everything
is going to be just perfect. So when things go wrong it is very
often utterly crushing. Most of the time there is absolutely
nothing you can do about a bad holiday. It is just bad luck
or – more commonly – your fault. You really should have
thought more carefully before booking that self-catering
caravan in Syria. You were warned! Sometimes, however,
when things go awry there are plenty of legal weapons you
can deploy to get your money back and additional compensation. Of all the legal issues in this book, the law relating to

holidays from hell is the most modern and consumer-friendly.

Judges deal with thousands of tales about holidays from hell in their courtrooms every year. Hotels described by travel agents as 'charming and quaint' turn out to be bullet-ridden shacks in the centre of a war zone. Children come away with E. coli and salmonella from the rotting cheese that they found being licked by local stray dogs on the hotel balcony, which their parents just assumed would be fine because it was on premises recommended by TripAdvisor. Passengers on low-budget airlines are dumped at an airport somewhere east of Slovenia for 14 hours and charged astronomical rates to visit the toilet, until they start using the bins instead. People cry, people lie and, occasionally, people even die.

Some are the fault of the idiots who booked the tours, and some are the fault of the idiots who ran them. Similarly, some complaints ('I was told I was staying in a boutique hotel in Paris, but when I got there it was a brothel') are completely justified, and some ('I woke up on the second day of my honeymoon and realised that my new bride was a dead ringer for Ursula the sea witch') are downright ridiculous. There are the overblown sob stories straight out of the mouths of a family of complete morons who have failed to scrape together a functioning brain cell between them in order to work out that an adventure holiday in Afghanistan sold to them by the *Big Issue* vendor down the road probably won't turn out to be the relaxing getaway they were pinning their hopes and dreams on. But then there are cases like the Beevers' recounted below, where people who should have received exactly what they paid for were instead given a nightmare of astronomical proportions.

HOLIDAY DISASTER STORIES

What happens if you're left sickened by the standards at your hotel (and not just because they play the 'Macarena' at full volume every three hours by the poolside and every other child in the kids' club is called Chardonnay)? While some holidays, like a fortnight in an under-30s resort in Magaluf, are deliberately planned to involve copious vomiting and the regular swapping of most other bodily fluids, the majority of people setting off abroad each year usually plan to avoid such an eventuality. Do you have any rights if you've spent most of your time getting closely acquainted with the U-bend of the en-suite toilet, rather than reclining under a waterfall in the sunshine? Or does the law have little sympathy for people who come back to the UK more run-down than when they set off?

Nightmare for the Beevers

The Beever family from Yorkshire were all set for their group vacation to the shores of Bulgaria. It had been a while since they'd managed to book a getaway together, and this time around, the whole 16 of them were looking forward to relaxing in the sunshine, bonding over all-inclusive cocktails, frolicking in the swimming pool, and generally not keeling over and throwing their guts up repeatedly into the hotel toilets. The sorts of things we all ideally wish for while on our holidays.

Unfortunately, the Black Sea resort that they arrived at fell slightly short of the mark. Cockroaches were found crawling along the floors in the bedrooms, while stagnant puddles of dirt were the norm around the communal areas, and flies munched happily alongside humans on the food in the buffet. One does slightly wonder why the Beevers kept coming back for more when they clocked that conditions at the resort were at an all-time hygiene low, but I suppose we were all optimists once.

Needless to say, almost every member of the family started suffering the unholy trinity of nausea, sickness and diarrhoea as soon as they walked away from the fly-infested ham sand-wiches, and it just kept on coming. The kids, two of whom were attempting (and spectacularly failing) to celebrate their birthdays, were particularly affected. Four years later, they were still suffering stomach cramps so debilitating that it kept them from participating in physical activities at school. Either that or they'd come up with the most inventive PE excuse ever.

THE VERDICT

The Beevers walked away from their ordeal with £119,000 compensation after a long legal battle, but they still had to live with long-lasting illnesses – something that really puts into perspective that nightmare time my entertainment system didn't work on the plane to Dubai. And that isn't the first or last time paying customers have won against holiday operators that prom-ised luxury and delivered the equivalent of a low-budget horror film: First Choice, Thomas Cook, Thomson and My Travel ended up collectively paying out more than £5 million to 1,000 unfortunate travellers in 2013 who had trusted them to deliver a high-class experience in the Dominican Republic but had instead been greeted with toilets flushing sewage backwards and one waiter literally keeling over and vomiting up his break-fast on the floor in reception. According to the guests in that case, ambulances appeared daily outside the hotel to ferry the sickest holidaymakers to the local hospital, so common were severe bouts of food poisoning – although, again, it's beyond us all why these families continued to merrily order their meals there while surrounded by the ailing bodies of the severely ill. Personally, a low score on Yelp can deter me from visiting a restaurant – but we all have our boundaries.

SO WHAT CAN I DO?

There are lots of ways you can deal with a desperately disastrous holiday. All is not lost and at the end of this chapter you'll find a list of things you can do, and failing that there's lots of advice on how to avoid it next time.

WHEN IS IT MY FAULT?

Then there are the holiday horrors that can't be attributed to anyone but the person who travelled there themselves. You might know a few people who could accurately be described as having maggots for brains – God knows I've encountered a few during my illustrious career in the legal profession.

Rochelle from Derby

Twenty-seven-year-old Rochelle Harris from Derby once quite literally ended up in this sorry situation after a seemingly lovely holiday in Peru. Having walked through a swarm of flies at one point during her vacation, she thought very little of it, although she did later mention that she remembered having to brush one of the flies out of her ear. A few weeks later, however, back home in the UK, she started to experience some rather mysterious and particularly excruciating headaches.

When these headaches progressed to shooting pains in her face, accompanied by an extremely unnerving scratching sound coming from inside her head, Rochelle decided that it might be time to discount her friends' advice that 'chilling out' and having a cup of tea would solve her ailments, and got herself down to A&E as fast as her little legs would carry her. After a full examination, it turned out that the news wasn't good: a family of Peruvian maggots had chewed 12mm into her ear canal, and it looked like they were determined to carry on tunnelling. After an emergency MRI scan showed that she was at risk of developing meningitis, paralysis or a fatal bleed on the brain thanks to the activities of the flesh-eating critters, doctors decided to deploy the least invasive method: attempting to drown the maggots by filling her ears with olive oil.

Unsurprisingly, this vain attempt at maggot-drowning failed, Rochelle woke up the next day with her ears still full of determined insects munching on the inside of her head. Thus followed a further, slightly more surgical, procedure, which did manage to rectify the problem, and Rochelle reports that she hasn't suffered any permanent after-effects from her toe-curlingly horrible ordeal. Regardless, I think I'll be crossing Machu Picchu off my bucket list.

THE VERDICT

In the case of Rochelle, no one could be held legally to blame: she'd chosen to visit a country where these sorts of insects are abundant, and no tour guide or holiday provider could have reasonably protected her. Her case does, however, highlight how important it is to take precautions when you venture a little further afield – and how important it is to take out comprehensive travel insurance, considering that if the maggots had started munching any sooner, while she was still on the ground in Peru, the medical expenses could have become impossibly high very, very quickly.

SO WHAT CAN I DO?

Sometimes it's nobody's fault that your holiday is a disaster. The best thing to do is to come to terms with this as soon as possible, and despite the trauma, try to enjoy your holiday. However, if you still feel that you want to consider your options as to what to do next, take a look at the golden Rinder's Rules at the end of this chapter.

WHEN IT'S REALLY BAD. . .

If you want to avoid a hotel-related disaster, then perhaps cruise ships are more your style. There's something undeniably liberating about taking a cruise: guaranteed sun, beautiful views, different beaches every few days, decadent parties at night, gorgeous sunsets across the water, kids' clubs, bingo nights for the grannies, smearing poo across the cabin walls, wading through rivers of urine in the dark on your way to the upper deck. Wait, what?

All aboard the Poop Cruise

Yes, it turns out that trouble can strike just as easily on a floating resort as it can on dry land – and, of course, when it does, there's quite literally no escape. Carnival Cruise Line used to be known for their luxurious getaways and vacation innovation. But then the revered *Carnival Triumph* cruise ship got stranded in the middle of the Gulf of Mexico after an engine fire, leaving 3,000 passengers floating on a ship without electricity and living off tiny supplies of food for five days. And everything changed, very quickly.

Spending your holiday on the *Carnival Triumph* turned out to be no mean feat: one guest on the ship described the atmosphere after lights went off, power failed and food became scarce as 'like *The Hunger Games*'. Yes, like the film where teenagers brutally murder each other for the entertainment of the nation, which I think it's fair to say is probably about the opposite of how anyone wants to end up describing their getaway to the family back home. People began hoarding food, terrified that they would starve at sea, and most passengers dragged their mattresses out of their cabins and outside on to the deck as the walls inside began to turn brown with raw running sewage. 'My toilet literally exploded,' one man memorably told the *Daily Mail*. Across the media, what used to be known as the provider of choice for lasting memories on beautiful boats became known as the Poop Cruise.

Pictures from the Poop Cruise are particularly grim to look through. Backed-up toilets and buckets along the corridors filled with suspicious brown liquid are the norm. Passengers hid under tables in the dining room as they tried to avoid the stench that filled the place. The dinner choices got whittled down to onion and cucumber sandwiches, and whole families started squatting over public bins and doing their business in front of everyone. One night, most passengers chose to sleep outside in the middle of a downpour rather than face the overpowering smell below deck that was produced after people started going to the toilet in their showers out of desperation. On Valentine's Day, they were served frozen waffles for their daily meal.

There's no doubt in everyone's minds that those who set off for sea on the *Carnival Triumph* were thinking more 'reclining by the pool with their sweetheart and a couple of margaritas' than 'nightly navigations of the diarrhoea slip slide' (a genuine description used by one woman when she stepped off the ship). Surely, then, the passengers who had become prisoners of their own poop had some legal recourse at the end of their horrifying ordeal?

THE VERDICT

The Poop Cruise was caused by an engine failure, which the operating company attempted to argue was an unforeseeable accident but was eventually ruled by a judge to be their fault. And that wasn't the end of this company's troubles: once they'd found themselves back on dry land in the world of 21st-century plumbing, 31 passengers formally sued in 2014, claiming that they had developed post-traumatic stress disorder and 'mental injuries' from the week. Lawsuits are still ongoing.

Admittedly it probably *isn't* that easy to forget the sight of people with whom you shared a civilised glass of expensive wine with over dinner squatting down and crapping in a bin next to you just 48 hours later – although most college students do tend to live perfectly happily with almost identical memories after freshers' week every single year. Considering what they'd been through, that horrifically unlucky set of passengers, some of whom had started to sleep outside in freezing rain rather than go back inside their floating sewage prison during their week at sea. But if all you've experienced is a room without a proper ocean view, then you're unlikely to be able to convince a judge that you're deserving of similar compensation.

SO WHAT CAN I DO?

Always stick by this rule of thumb: if you came away feeling similar to how you would have felt on the Poop Cruise, then know your rights and get yourself to court. If not, reassess whether you've really got your priorities straight. Either way, read on to find out exactly what you can and should do in the event that things go horribly wrong!

TERRIBLE FLIGHTS

But a person like *you* wouldn't set foot on a cruise liner in the first place, I hear you cry. You're a high-flyer after all, quite literally, and all of your choice destinations are reachable by plane. A floating, sewage-ridden ocean liner just isn't your bag. You'll be laughing sadistically at the stranded form of the Poop Cruise as you recline on your private beach in Cancún, after a relaxing flight with a very reasonable budget airline only hours before.

Or will you? Because if one party of unfortunate sun-seekers are anything to go by, you may be waiting to reach that dream destination for a while.

Airline trouble

After storms hit the island of Corfu in October 2014, a number of Ryanair flights were cancelled, leaving 40 passengers claiming to the *Mirror* that they had stayed in the airport for 72 hours. According to the 40 unfortunates, all the other airlines were still happily flying their planes in and out of the island. Many broke down in tears while waiting in line. The chief executive of Ryanair, Michael O'Leary, a delightfully outspoken gentleman known for his complete lack of love or respect for his staff or his passengers, once famously told one of his more disgruntled customers: 'You're getting no refund so f*** off. We don't want to hear your sob stories. What part of "no refund" don't you understand?' and claimed that all Ryanair planes 'are fuelled with leprechaun wee and my bullshit'. He also suggested that pilots should ramp up the turbulence to impact positively on booze sales, and described the infamous Ryanair service thus: 'Anyone who thinks that Ryanair flights are some bastion of sanctity where you contemplate your navel is wrong. We already bombard you with as many in-flight announcements and trolleys as we can. Anyone who looks like sleeping, we wake them up to sell them things.' Delightful!

THE VERDICT

The supposedly friendlier side of budget flying, EasyJet, whose chief executive has never once referred to a plane-load of her passengers as 'wankers', has nevertheless paid out a wad of compensation in the past – most notably to one family who turned up at the airport at the end of their holiday to find that their flight was cancelled because the pilot of the plane wasn't actually qualified to fly one. The man's licence had expired, leaving the family of four and a half (one of them was pregnant) to fork out £800 to fly home with a different airline three days later, rather than wait another week for EasyJet to find its own replacement.

Still feeling snooty? Even the well-respected UK flag carrier British Airways once left 38 of their holidaymakers on the airport floor in Mumbai after a flight connection went wrong – and they only ended up getting on a rescheduled one after some tech-savvy travellers staged a 36-hour-long Twitter protest. One of the hapless passengers left to sleep on the tiles for two days was Sean Read, the keyboard player for the Manic Street Preachers. Bet he wished he'd just bitten the bullet and gone with Ryanair for his hassle, especially considering that O'Leary recently claimed that he would personally wipe a passenger's bottom if they paid £5 to use the toilet on one of his aeroplanes, and I'm sure Sean isn't short of a few spare fivers.

SO WHAT CAN I DO?

If you're left stranded in an airport or unable to leave your destination, you do have rights – and it's best to know them, because some airlines will try and wriggle out of them if they can. These vary according to which country you're in, and exactly why you're stuck there ('acts of God', like the famous Icelandic volcano that grounded hundreds of flights across Europe in 2010, aren't seen as the fault of the operators – but pilots forgetting their licences or companies overselling your tickets certainly are). Find out at the end of the chapter how best to approach airlines in the event that something awful happens to you.

Judge Rinder's holiday hell

I too have had my share of holiday horror. I had just finished defending in a particularly grim murder case at the Old Bailey and desperately needed a – perfectly understandable – break away from crime scenes, dead bodies and psychopathic clients. Having tolerated my mild lunacy during the trial, which had reached a particularly crazed low, my poor partner suggested that I visit an exorcist; I thought a trip to Tuscany would do the trick instead. What could be more relaxing than a 'private castle' in the most beautiful part of the Italian countryside (as the website promised)? We arrived at a debris-strewn concrete driveway which looked like a homage to Berlin after the war and discovered a building which was less 'castle' and more 'bungalow with bits added by Blue Peter competition winners'. We were greeted by an ancient woman with designer facial stubble who shuffled to our room. Finding the key was a challenge for the poor dear, who had more metal on her belt than a crypt keeper (which is where I suspect she visited her friends each night). After forcing the woodwormed door open we were met with something which resembled the murder scene from the case I had just been working on. We had been promised 'heavenly luxury'; we were given 'Romanian prison'.

During the course of the rest of the trip, I met a seemingly thoughtful pharmacist who suggested that I try out some carrot-based sun-tanning oil: 'Itsa gooda fora the skina,' she said in her best Italian–English. Not being able to read the instructions (which were, I think, in some kind of Serbo-Croat), I put what I considered to be a reasonable amount on and had a gentle nap in the sun. I woke up to discover that my face looked as if it had been on a package holiday to Chernobyl. Worse still, when I returned to court the following week I could not rid myself of the orange hue, which was particularly disastrous as, in combination with the white barrister's wig, I looked uncannily like one of Roald

Dahl's Oompa Loompas – a look I sported for well over a month, much to the amusement of my colleagues who rather imaginatively started delivering anonymous donations of Tango to my chambers.

SO WHAT CAN I DO?

- Most problems are identified on the first day of the holiday: you were seated in economy instead of premium economy, which you had paid for; you had to wait four hours for the transfer car from the airport; the hotel was cockroach- and rat-infested with major building work being conducted.

- You should contact the package organiser, who will usually be your tour operator, but who also may be your travel agent. They may have a representative at your holiday resort, but also may only be contactable by email or telephone in the UK (see Rinder's Rules below).

- You should identify the problems as soon as possible and give them the opportunity to put right what they can, e.g. by moving you to a new hotel or ensuring your transfers are in place and that you have the correct seats on the return flight. You should take photographs; obtain contact details of other guests who, similarly let down, can corroborate what you have experienced; keep records of all conversations with the company, a diary of when and how the problem affected you, and records of all additional expense.

- If you cannot contact the tour company, you should retain the evidence of your efforts to do so. You can, if you have the wherewithal, find alternative accommodation yourself, keeping comprehensive records of all expense incurred and receipts.

- Under package travel regulations your organiser has a responsibility to make sure that you get the holiday you paid for. Even if your package organiser has contracts with others (e.g. the airline, the transfer company and the hotel) to provide the different parts of your holiday, the organiser is responsible.

- If the local representative cannot resolve your issues, complain to the organiser's head office in the UK. The representative should provide you with a complaints form. If they do not give you a form, write a letter of complaint and ask them to sign it. Ensure you have a copy of the letter or form. You will need to take your complaint further when you get home. (See what to include in this letter below.)

- If you paid any part of the cost of your holiday by credit card you might be able to make a claim against the credit-card company under Section 75 of the Consumer Credit Act 1974.

- If your organiser is a member of a trade association like the Association of British Travel Agents (ABTA) or the Association of Independent Tour Operators (AITO) they may be able to resolve issues.

- You can register your complaint with the trade association, providing them with your documentation and evidence supporting your complaint and claim for compensation. If they cannot resolve the issues, they can supply details of an independent arbitration service. However, you must pay for the service and it then precludes you from taking the holiday company to court.

- If you do not receive satisfaction and you still feel strongly that the holiday organiser has let you down in contravention of the Consumer Protection from Unfair Trading Regulations and/or the Supply of Goods and Services Act 1982, finish reading this chapter and consider taking them to court.

- For the law relating to missed or cancelled flights – see the Appendix at the end of this book.

RINDER'S RULES

- Try to deal with the problem while you are there.

- Get your first complaint right.

- Be persistent and sue the morons.

- Don't be a total fool! ALWAYS BUY TRAVEL INSURANCE BEFORE YOU LEAVE THE COUNTRY.

Deal with the problem straight away

- In many instances, small issues can be resolved by the operator, agent, hotelier or owner while you're still on holiday. Any claim you may bring in the future will be greatly assisted if you have given them the opportunity to put things right. You must remember to be fair and realistic. While you are perfectly entitled to an air-conditioning unit which doesn't keep you up all night making gurgling noises, you cannot grumble if, having booked a room with a sea view, you don't like the quality of the boats that sail past.

- Make sure you identify the person who can actually do something for you. There is no point screaming at the receptionist; she is probably working for minimum wage and hasn't slept for a week. Simply ask calmly to speak to the manager. Do not be fobbed off by excuses that the boss is in some sort of meeting. Wait! Explain that you want the problem fixed at once and decide – before you begin the discussion – exactly what compensation you think would be reasonable. You need to be fair about this. You cannot demand an entire refund for the trip because you don't approve of the colour of the bedspread but you should be upset when plumbing doesn't work or your room has been inadequately cleaned.

- Remember you are legally entitled to everything that was described to you when you booked the holiday. In the event that you don't get a satisfactory response, keep evidence of everything. And for goodness' sake, do not forget to take photos. I love a good photo in my court!

Get your first complaint right

- Finding the correct person to direct your complaint to can be difficult these days as most of us organise holidays through faceless websites.

- Don't waste time sending junk mail to some lowly office flunkey; get the letter to the head of the company.

- Keep your complaint simple by focusing on the main issues and explaining why you feel the contract or booking conditions have been breached. Naturally you should include any evidence you have.

- For heaven's sake, make sure you clearly set out exactly what you want. There is nothing more unhelpful – not to mention off-putting – than a 200-page novel about your diphtheria. Get to the point. Be clear about how you have come to the figure you are claiming for.

- Government websites and Citizens Advice Bureau can help with this. Demand a reply within 28 days and make it clear that you intend to take them to court if they don't pay up.

Be persistent and sue the morons

- Do not accept a low-ball offer. So long as your claim is reasonable you are entitled to full compensation. In the event that you do not receive a satisfactory outcome, you have a number of options. You could take the holiday company to the small claims court, which – as I keep repeating – is extremely easy. You will have the chance to put your case in front of a judge without a lawyer, which is not only cheaper but, in most cases, far better. Judges are often just like me: thoughtful, patient and trained to smell the lies and excuses of big companies.

- If you want to try a less contentious route, you could use the arbitration services of the two main trade associations, ABTA and AITO, which will decide your case based solely on the evidence you provide them with. If you win you will receive the money very quickly. There are very specific rules that apply to these services, which you must carefully check before going ahead.

- If you have paid up front for a private villa in a foreign country you have about as much chance of getting your money back from a reluctant owner as finding me jumping out of an aircraft dressed as Judy Garland while doing jazz hands (i.e. only a very small chance). If you end up in dispute with some belligerent guest-house owner in the UK then take them to the small claims court or bring them before me. I'm sure I'll just love hearing why the owner thinks filthy sheets are refugee-chic and completely safe to sleep in.

- A holiday contract will also include some terms and conditions which consumer law makes automatically part of the contract. These are called implied terms. The most common implied term in a holiday contract is that any service you receive must be carried out with reasonable care and skill (Supply of Goods and Services Act

1982). This would include your entitlement to expect your holiday accommodation to be clean and in a reasonable state of repair. If this is not the case, you could claim that your holiday contract hasn't been carried out with reasonable care and skill and get your money back.

CHAPTER 3

PETS

To say that we love our pets in this country is a Great Dane-sized understatement. To date in 2015, we Britons have spent £7.16 billion on our pets. Yes, you read that correctly! That is more than the Gross Domestic Product of a significant number of sub-Saharan countries. The amount of money and love we invest in our pets perhaps explains why of all the cases I see in my court, legal wrangles over beloved animals are the most contentious and, in many instances, the most legally complicated. I am an unashamed dog-lover and – as anyone who has seen the programme knows – often wipe the floor with negligent pet owners. The reality, however, is that whether we love our pets or not, as you will discover in this chapter, they have no higher status in law than any other property, which is completely outrageous and causes real emotional distress when things go wrong. In this chapter you will learn what to do in the event that you share a pet with a partner and you break up, what to do if your pet is lost or stolen, and how best to manage a situation where your animal injures somebody. Anyone who has ever owned a pet, or is even contemplating buying one, should READ ON!

PET CUSTODY

Custody battles are always difficult, but usually that's because children are involved. However, nowadays the classic parental battle about where little Oscar will spend the weekend getting interrogated about Mummy's new boyfriend are so passé. An equal amount of acrimony has begun to occur in rows about where Joey will end up chewing his brand-new bone instead.

Shannon's case: the canine soulmate

Shannon Travis and Trisha Murray started out very much in love. They got married, moved in to a charming apartment in New York together, and bought a miniature dachshund called Joey to seal the deal. That should have been the end of the fairy tale, but unfortunately, the path of true love never did run smooth. Shannon went on a business trip a year after she and Trisha were wed, and when she returned, Trisha had disappeared – with Joey in tow. Well, Shannon wasn't going to put up with that sort of behaviour after she'd been slaving away for the benefit of the marriage. In true Wicked Witch of the West style, she vowed that she'd get back at her partner, and get her little dog back too.

And so began a landmark matrimonial custody battle: the two dog-loving women dragged their divorce case through the Manhattan courtrooms, fighting tooth and nail over who would get the privilege of living with Joey after the break-up. Trisha stood up as the case was threatening to close and made an emotional speech about why she shouldn't be separated from the dog, presumably mistaking her turn in the court of law for a solo in an episode of *Glee*.

'I consider this puppy, my little angel Joey, the love of my life,' she stated, remaining entirely deadpan. 'He is my soulmate, and there is no way in this lifetime that I could ever live without him.'

Yes, a married woman stood up in a serious legal setting during divorce proceedings and announced to all of those present that the family dog was her soulmate. And you thought your last relationship had issues!

So should it be taken into account that Trisha loved Joey so much she was willing to publicly declare him her soulmate, at the clear expense of her dignity? Do love and care hold real sway in the courtroom where pets are involved, as they can do with children? Is Joey, in fact, even seen in the eyes of the law as a person-like creature capable of benefiting from this love, or just another piece of property to be divided up between the couple (hopefully not literally)? What would have happened to Joey if his owners had been fighting over him in the UK? And are Joey's best interests the business of a family court judge anyway?

In some ways, this all makes logical sense. After all, Oscar will grow up to be a spotty, foul-mouthed, ungrateful teenager who will slam doors, call you names, bring home girlfriends with eyebrow piercings and insatiable sex drives, and leave used condoms down the back of the sofa the next morning. Joey will stay the same furry little ball of devotion, greeting you happily at the front door every day after work, and if he ever gets a bit temperamental then you can have him neutered in a routine operation. Try that with Oscar and you'll end up needing a barrister! Quick fixes just don't exist with kids.

THE VERDICT

In the case of Trisha, Shannon and Joey, it's clear that Joey is much more than property to the two defendants, even if the law doesn't strictly see it that way. Even though both US and UK law say that any pet has about as many rights as a coffee table, judges are sometimes allowed to use their discretion – and this one did. Shannon argued that she'd used her own money to buy Joey, and so she should automatically be given Joey in the same way that she might be given a DVD or a piece of jewellery she'd bought from a shop. But in the end, lawyers didn't see it all as that straightforward.

When parents divorce and enter custody battles over children, a judge is supposed to prioritise what is in 'the best interests of the child'. This means that Oscar is supposed to live with someone who will provide the best kind of life for him, who has a close bond with him and who has some sort of advantage over the other partner – a state-of-the-art city apartment next to the best school in London, for instance, rather than a 'charmingly quaint' shack made of sticks on a beach in Cornwall with a dreadlocked Buddhist convert father who's into homeschooling. Oscar would be placed in the most appropriate home, regardless of how much it might hurt one of the parents, because his interests are seen as more important than those of the divorcing couple.

The judge in the case of Shannon, Trisha and Joey thought it might be taking it a bit far to prioritise 'the best interests of the dog' above the effect on the human couple in the same way that you might do with a child. (As one legal mastermind pointed out during the case, the major difference is that 'a child is a human being and a dog is a domestic animal'. The things they teach at law school these days are evidently pushing boundaries.) Instead, he ruled that they should use a principle of 'the best interests for all' – meaning that the court would have to ask questions like: who provides food, shelter and vets' fees for Joey? Who is more likely to benefit from having Joey in her life? And who has Joey been spending most of his time with? This meant that Joey ended up as legally a bit more than a DVD box set of *Friends* and a bit less than a human child, potentially changing how further cases might be dealt with in future.

SO WHAT CAN I DO?

At the end of this section, I will go through the stages of what you can do to successfully deal with the issue of pet custody. So make sure you read on. . .

PET MAINTENANCE

Can a person claim 'pet maintenance', in the way that child maintenance is routine? Is it reasonable to keep three horses, at vast expense, because your hobby of eventing is close to your heart, if your husband was the breadwinner throughout the marriage? And is this really a straightforward case of cash, or something that requires a little bit more nuance?

Bill and Jane and her beloved horses

Bill and Jane were a couple who lived in luxury. They met when Bill was just starting out as a banker and Jane was working part-time in the financial sector: a power couple if ever there was one. They gallivanted around London, flashing the cash, for a few years before deciding that they'd prefer to be big fish in a small pond and settling down in a country estate in Gloucestershire. Jane quit her job, became the kind of curtain-twitching housewife who talks loudly about the poor quality of quiche at the church bake sale and the declining value of Aston Martins these days, and kicked back in their shared Cotswold mansion for a decade-long rest. Bill continued to climb the ranks in City banking, equally comfortable to be the sort of obnoxious fool who shouts into his iPhone in the quiet carriage and acts as though you told him his baby was ugly if you ask him to lower his voice. In other words, they should have been perfect for each other, for ever.

Unfortunately, it all fell apart. Jane tired of the country, and Bill tired of Jane; divorce proceedings began, and assets began to be divided up. The split was a nasty one, with Bill claiming that he would strip Jane of any 'unnecessary luxury' in her life. Included in what he saw as 'unnecessary luxury' was her impressive collection of three show horses, one of which he had bought for her as a foal on their tenth wedding anniversary. He suggested that Jane keep one and put it into livery, while finding herself a new full-time job. Jane had other ideas, and argued that the horses were essentially surrogate children to her, meaning that she would be due maintenance for their upkeep and enough money to support all three.

THE VERDICT

Money didn't buy Bill and Jane happiness, but the judge in this case ruled that it might be able to buy lasting happiness for Jane after the marriage was dissolved. The horses, he argued, were such a big part of Jane's life that he agreed they should be seen as equally important as children would have been.

Jane walked away with a £1.5-million divorce deal, which included a £50,000-a-year maintenance package for all three horses. The court's decision hinged on the fact that if she kept all three horses, she would have to buy a home with enough land to house them, and since the show horses and Jane's hobby of eventing were central to her life during the 11 years of her marriage to Bill, she had the right to hold on to them – even if Bill no longer wanted to hold on to her.

Some divorce lawyers were horrified by this decision. 'Pet maintenance' isn't a real legal term and it isn't something that Jane's legal team were able to draw from, but that was what a large chunk of her divorce package boiled down to. People loudly complained that the whole family justice system would be upset if pets started taking on equal standing in a judge's mind to children – and they're right. But maybe it's a change that needs to happen.

SO WHAT CAN I DO?

Whatever our feelings about our beloved animals, the law in the UK considers pets to be nothing more than property. Your dog or cat has no more value in a break-up than a set of hair straighteners. If you think that's outrageous then you are entirely right! Although the judge in Shannon's case attempted to find a creative legal solution, when an animal is the subject of litigation, in most instances the court will simply regard the dispute as being one about a piece of property. In other words, judges will ask themselves the following two questions: who is more entitled to it and who owns the thing? If you break up with your partner and there is an animal involved (yes, I mean the pet!) then your primary duty is to attempt to put aside your desire to have your ex neutered and act like a grown-up.

Sadly, in the UK we are still way behind the US when it

comes to dealing with cases of this kind. We probably love our pets more than any other nation on the planet. Think about it! Force a celebrity into a jungle with nothing more than an elastic band and a kangaroo-anus sandwich for a month then subject them to ritualised humiliation and tens of millions of us will cheer them on with glee. Show a hamster on telly at teatime without the 'correct food', on the other hand, and thousands of us will write in demanding justice!

- The first thing you should do if possible is to determine who can give the best home to the animal. It is one thing moving a dog to a new territory, but rehoming a cat can be deeply stressful to the animal. You should attempt to devise a written access agreement or consent order between you which sets out exactly who can see the pet and when, and then *both* sign it. Although this agreement would not be legally enforceable, it often works.

- Try mediation. This means appointing an independent, professionally trained third party who can help with the negotiations, minimising both cost and conflict. The addition of an independent party means that hopefully your meeting won't dissolve into screaming and shouting and a decision might actually be made. Mediation gives everyone involved an opportunity to be heard and helps identify a constructive way forward in a more formal, structured environment. This can often be cheaper than proceedings in court, and in any event, you must show to the court (if you do go down that route) that you have at least attempted to solve the problem. Your county court or local Citizens Advice Bureau might be able to put you in contact with mediators.

- As a pet is only property in the eyes of the law (as I keep reminding you), you could go to the small claims court to demand full ownership or – worse still – be taken to court. See my guide in Chapter 12 for help on how to bring a case to the small claims court. In cases like this the court will consider a number of factors in order to determine who owns the animal, such as:
1. Who bought the pet in the first place?
2. Who has done most to feed and maintain the animal?
3. What is in the best interests of the health of the pet?

RINDER'S RULES

- If I had a pound for every time I was asked a question about pet custody I could finally purchase that new electric chair I've been after for my courtroom in which I would place animal abusers and deadbeat dads. I wouldn't harm them of course; just a little jolt. . . Nothing lethal! Every time I am asked a question like this I say the same thing. If you love your animal, act like a human! Put your animals first and your feelings last.

- Going to court in any circumstances can be incredibly stressful so you should attempt to avoid it at all costs. If you can't agree on who gets the pet then for goodness' sake attempt to mediate.

- Get a consent order like the one I described above.

- Offer to replace the pet with a new animal. I know it seems heartless.

- Make sure you keep a record after your break-up of everything you have done for the animal – it will help your case in the event that you are forced to go to court.

- Gather evidence. If your neighbours saw that you were always the one who walked the dog, they may be useful witnesses who can confirm your consistent interaction with the animal and therefore be helpful to your case.

ILLEGAL PET NAMES

A dog named Itler

Louis (name changed to protect the idiotic) had been ruminating over what to call his two new American Staffordshire terriers for weeks. What was the sort of image he wanted to project as a dog owner he wondered. What would perfectly sum up his outlook, his lifestyle and his affection for his two adorable furballs of joy? What would distinguish his playful canine pals from the crowd in parks full of everyday Rovers, Butches and Fidos, because Lord knows it's hard for a dog to stand out in the world these days? Louis delved into the murky recesses of his mind, and after searching the shockingly shallow depths of his IQ for what one presumes was a difficult couple of minutes, he came up with the perfect answer: Itler and Iva.

Now, it doesn't take a genius to work out that the particular names bear a striking resemblance to the names of Adolf Hitler and his wife Eva Braun. It's fair to say that most people would have found the combination distasteful, but one person – the mayor of the small town of St-Nicolas-de-Port, where Louis and his pooches lived – took particularly active offence.

THE VERDICT

Strangely enough, Mayor Luc Binsinger didn't think it would reflect well on his quaint town in the east of France if tourists and passers-by were treated to a resident dog walker running after his Staffie yelling, 'Heel, Itler!' Clearly, this man was blessed with a bit more intelligence and foresight than Louis, whom we might kindly describe as the village idiot. Mr Binsinger vowed to do everything in his power to prevent Itler and Iva from disgracing the local green – but could he, as a mere small-town mayor, actually hold any sway in this situation? Is a pet's name the business of the owner and nobody else, even if it's in danger of bringing the whole town into disrepute? Can you really force an owner to change his dogs' names?

The usual answer to this question would be no. We have no specific laws in the UK relating to what you name your cat, dog, snake or hamster, and even our laws on what you name your children are very lax. In some countries, human names are strictly controlled: Argentina, Germany, Portugal and Spain have a list of officially sanctioned names that you have to choose your baby's moniker from, and other countries can be fairly strict. In early 2015, a French court prevented one couple from calling their daughter Nutella and legally renamed her Ella, because the French have no sense of humour and very little appreciation for the best spread ever brought into existence.

SO WHAT CAN I DO?

As far as the UK is concerned, almost anything goes, unless the name specifically promotes an extremely offensive viewpoint that would cause significant distress to the child and those around them (Hitler, Pol Pot, Fascist or Cocaine are a few prominent examples). According to official records, there are a fair few British children wandering around with the names Superman, Gandalf, Gazza and Arsenal, which really does highlight the fact that becoming a parent is the job with the lowest qualification requirement going (Oh, you know how to thrust? Here, take a human for ever!). Nevertheless, in the UK we like our liberties, and any attempt to limit the Supermen and the Gandalfs would probably be met with staunch opposition.

If you come across a pair of dogs called Itler and Iva in Newcastle, Nottingham or Northamptonshire then, you'll just have to suck it up and do what British people do best: tut loudly and make silent judgements about the character of the person you're tutting at.

LOST PETS

The thing most pet owners dread the most is their beloved pet going missing. In most cases they return after a night/day out on the town but sometimes when they go missing they really do go missing. Here's what to do if this happens to you.

Wellie's case

Wellie, a wire-haired terrier, belonged to a 14-year-old boy in Somerset. Wellie and Tom were the best of friends, spending days together in each other's company, taking long walks on the beach, cuddling up on the couch over romantic movies and generally undertaking all of the other activities a young boy and his dog might enjoy. They lived in a veritable utopia of pet-based joy.

And then, like all good things, the utopia came to an end. Wellie disappeared and Tom was left heartbroken, calling round local shelters, vets' surgeries and the RSPCA to no avail. Unbeknown to him, however, one of the shelters he'd missed had taken in the dog, waited a few days and then dutifully rehomed him. Within a week, Wellie was living with a new family just down the road.

When Tom and his family found out about the mix-up, they thought that a quick phone call about a little boy who couldn't wait to be reunited with his childhood pal would sort everything out. But, despite the fact that rescue dogs are supposed to be the red-headed stepchildren of the animal world, the new owners decided that they had inextricably bonded with Wellie – and they weren't giving him up without a fight.

In this sort of situation, what is the original owner supposed to do? Is there any legal recourse that you can take? Or was Wellie gone for ever, presumably taking Tom's childlike optimism about the world with him?

THE VERDICT

In this case, Tom's family didn't take the Wellie situation lying down: they instructed a solicitor to start legal action against the

---

council who ran the animal centre, as well as the kennels themselves. No gentle negotiation for this family – they were going in with all guns blazing, and they were going to get the hostage out. Their complaint centred on the idea that their property had been stolen without their knowledge, and then resold without their consent.

A few weeks passed, and eventually Tom did get his happy ending. The new owners of Wellie claimed to be so exasperated with the constant legal onslaught that they did something no grown adult ever wants to do: they gave the lost puppy back to the lonesome little boy. Tom's family withdrew their threat of legal action, but told the BBC – because of course the BBC was involved by this point – that they would try to recoup the costs lost during meetings with their solicitor. The tug of war over Wellie had come to an end, but not a particularly friendly one.

SO WHAT CAN I DO?

Your pet insurance should cover any expenses you incur while attempting to find your pet (see what I think of uninsured pet owners in the next section). In the meantime you are entitled to do anything *reasonable* to get your property back; that doesn't mean that you are allowed to hire Magnum PI or get Poirot on the job then pass on the expense to the insurer!

If you find that your pet has been taken and it wasn't your fault (as in Tom's case) a sweet knock at the door and a letter explaining the impact the loss of the animal has had on you and the family normally works a treat. Better still, it avoids the ugliness and unnecessary expense of lawyers.

THE BITING PET

Anybody who has watched my courtroom cases knows that I love animals and have little time for the dimbos who purchase them without proper thought or concern. It is particularly objectionable, for instance, when some moron purchases a dog thinking it was 'only going to be teacup-sized' and then attempts to return it when the pooch turns out to be a real dog as opposed to a hair accessory with eyes.

Judge Rinder's dog

Several years ago my beloved – if slightly bonkers – Jack Russell, Albert, was being walked by my particularly wonderful aunt in a local park. Albert was by no means an angel. He would, for example, bark at fat men and people on bicycles. I always considered this to be some sort of doggy public-service broadcast. After all, I suspect many people could do with the benefit of having a dog bark at them every time they are tempted by that one last chocolate button!

On this particular day, Albert had the misfortune of meeting a local Labrador who had recently been released from quarantine (it was before the days of pet passports). To most people Labradors are rather like sweet gentle children who like nothing more than kissing little babies and running round the house with soft loo-roll in their jaws. The fact is, however, like any animal, improperly trained and allowed to get out of control, your benign pet can become lethal in seconds. This Lab took a particular dislike to Albert and after an initial bottom-sniff picked Albert up in its mouth, breaking his spine and causing a range of other injuries resulting in Albert's death. My aunt was – to say the least – completely distraught. The owner of the Lab offered to pay for a new dog, which was about as welcome and sensitive an offer as a chef offering to prepare a pork supper for my bar mitzvah. The matter was ultimately reported to the police, who took no action against the owner of the Lab. Happily I had pet insurance so the bills for Albert's emergency treatment were covered. The trauma to my aunt, however, lives on.

RINDER'S RULES

- Anyone who has ever observed my courtroom knows that I take pet-on-pet violence extremely seriously. For the avoidance of any doubt, when one animal attacks another it is *nearly always* the owner's fault.

- You are required by law to have control over your property, which means that if your animal goes berserk it is your responsibility.

- If you or another person has been bitten by someone else's pet, call the police! In all likelihood the owner has committed a criminal offence.

- There is no law requiring you to have pet insurance but there jolly well ought to be and, frankly, if you don't have it then you are, in my view, not a responsible owner. You may love your pets but you have to pay for them, and if they do damage that could be extremely costly indeed.

- If your dog is off a lead and has bitten another animal

you must leave your name and address and offer to pay for any damage at once. Don't be a coward and wait to be found. The police are likely to be less sympathetic to you and, worse still, you'll cause serious distress to the other family.

• If your animal has an aggressive disposition, then you are legally 'on notice' that the dog is a risk and should be on a lead with a muzzle. Don't be a *moron*. This is not cruel or unfair to the dog. It is *your* responsibility to ensure the safety of other animals, not to mention people, and if your dangerous dog was unmuzzled and off its lead a court (particularly my court) is likely to throw the gavel at you faster than you can say 'woof'!

CHAPTER 4

BAD NEIGHBOURS

Many cases involving bad neighbours are clear-cut: there is one inconsiderate thug in the area who is completely indifferent to everybody else. You almost certainly know the type I am referring to: think of head-banging music played until 3am and a dog who treats your front doorstep as a litter tray and you have the idea! Not all cases involving neighbourhood disputes are this black and white, however. Very often, when neighbours end up in a squabble, it is six of one and half a dozen of the other. In other words, the parties have fallen out over a long period of time and have an equal share of complaints against each other. Whether you live next door to a belligerent moron or you have a more complex dispute, read on! In this chapter you will hear some extraordinary tales of local clashes and will learn what to do if you end up saddled with a neighbour from hell. Pay attention to my rules at the end. In nearly all cases these disputes can be resolved without going to court. As you will discover (and hopefully learn) you should do everything you possibly can to avoid taking legal action. Taking your neighbour to court should only ever be something you do as an absolute last resort.

UNRULY NEIGHBOURS

Most of us have had to put up with a Category A moron at some stage of our lives. Perhaps it's a colleague or boss at work, or perhaps even someone masquerading as a friend. Perhaps it's your mother-in-law, or your local MP.

Vile Gordon

On a particularly balmy summer day in 2010, Lara Sanger was reading a book in her bedroom in Crawley, West Sussex, when a sudden waft of stinking smoke came in through the window. Your first reaction to reading that might be 'Nice try, Lara – most people just end up blaming it on the dog,' but Sanger knew this time around that something bad was afoot. She'd been living next door to 52-year-old Gordon Clarke for some time, and he didn't exactly have the best reputation for community relations – he had, in fact, even starred in the TV programme *Neighbours From Hell* a few years earlier in 1995. That fact alone might have tipped off the residents on Lara's street that they weren't about to share their friendly terrace with a guy who helps you shovel snow off your lawn and brings round fresh cookies 'just because'.

Lara was a smart girl, and she knew there's no smoke without fire – so she shut her windows because the thick, dark stink was continuing to pour into her house. It wasn't just going into her garden and the immediate surroundings either. 'It was going round the whole neighbourhood,' she said in court, when she eventually managed to bring the culprit to (some version of) justice. 'There was a blanket of smoke across the gardens.'

Now, a fair few readers out there might defend Gordon Clarke's right to light a bonfire in his own garden. We've all enjoyed burning a pile of leaves and some wood on the fifth of November, or occasionally lighting up some garden waste away from the house. Unfortunately, Gordon wasn't the sort of man who lights bonfires for the joy of children or because his gardening work is done. Gordon was, instead, the sort of man who comes out during funeral processions on the street and claps. Loudly. This is just one of a catalogue of bizarre behaviours that he is on record as actually having carried out. In other words, ladies and gentlemen, Gordon Clarke was a Category A moron.

After he'd set off his first smoky bonfire, he then shouted out to all the neighbours in the surrounding area that he was going to set off an 'extra smoky' one tomorrow. And, although he denied it in the courtroom, all of his fellow residents claimed that he added chunks of plastic to his bonfires so that the smoke making its way through their windows and into their gardens was toxic.

Why would somebody go to such deliberate lengths to annoy their neighbours? Nobody quite knows why Gordon was driven to cause everyone around him abject irritation, but his literal partner in crime made it clear that that's exactly what they were trying to do. During filming for the documentary made about hellish neighbours in the nineties, his wife Jay Clarke happily claimed that she had bought a goat, painted her house pink, and looked into buying loudly crowing cockerels 'just to annoy locals'. And yes, you heard that right: Gordon the coffin-applauding plastic-burner was married. The man who apparently jumped out from street corners and shouted 'Paedophile!' at people speaking to children had managed to convince another human being to walk down the aisle and commit her life to him.

To be fair to Gordon, it does appear that he married his perfect match. Only a woman with a goat she didn't want, who painted her house a colour she didn't actually like, and wanted to buy cockerels that would seriously inconvenience her own life, solely in order to upset other people, would suit our friend Mr Clarke. Other fantastic quirks of his behaviour included following his neighbours round with a camera and taking their picture constantly 'as if he were paparazzi', which I'm sure we can all agree might be delightfully exciting for a day but probably became less amusing after a week. He also kept 12 dogs in his back yard – presumably because the goat was lonely – and encouraged them to bark continuously at all hours. None of this compares to the two most stand-out antisocial behaviours he exhibited though: shooting air rifles at residents (because how else do you bring variety and a new lease of life to a sleepy suburban neighbourhood poised on the brink of becoming mundane?), and reacting to the news that one of his neighbours had a terminal illness by loudly and obnoxiously singing the Queen song 'Another One Bites the Dust'.

THE VERDICT

Did Gordon ever get called to task for his Category A moronic behaviour then? Well, he did – but it didn't really seem to deter him. In 1998 he went to prison for harassment, in 2001 he was back inside for violating a restraining order, and in 2008 the same thing happened again. Not one to learn from past mistakes, he merely upped the ante and kept merrily bonfiring his way to another court case. In 2010 he'd been legally ordered to stop lighting bonfires and given an ASBO preventing him from being abusive towards the street's residents (something most of us don't need an ASBO to work out, but some people are late bloomers). He was also told to attend counselling sessions to find out exactly why he wanted to choke everyone around him with toxic fumes, which sounds both fairly sensible and a little bit lenient. Some of his Crawley neighbours, funnily enough, thought that Gordon deserved a bit more than a tearful hug from a therapist when he made a breakthrough about his father after causing them all misery for more than 20 years of their lives.

In 2012 the *Daily Mail* reported that Gordon had been found guilty, once again, of harassment without violence, before the case was adjourned for a pre-sentence report. Nobody felt particularly convinced that he was finished with his lifetime commitment to aggravating the hell out of everyone who had the audacity to live nearby.

SO WHAT CAN I DO?

So did Gordon Clarke deserve what he got? – or did he deserve a lot more (and we're talking within the boundaries of the law here)? Why did he end up with a restraining order and an ASBO when it was clear that he was all too happy to violate both? Can a person who is causing persistent nuisance to a community just end up going in and out of prison on minor offences, forever to return to the scene of the crime to start buying goats and singing mean songs in public to the terminally ill once again? And if you're faced with a neighbour like Gordon, what's the most effective way you can boot him out of his cosy situation next to you and into another street, off to cause misery to some other family entirely? Read my rules at the end of this chapter to find out exactly how!

NOISY NEIGHBOURS

We all know that at some point in our lives we will have to have neighbours, unless your names are David and Victoria

Beckham, in which case noisy neighbours is pretty low down on your list of woes.

Steve and Caroline

Steve and his wife Caroline were a passionate couple who had clearly managed to keep the spark alive in their long-term relationship, so much so that they were dedicated to late-night lovemaking at the expense of pretty much everybody around them. One woman, who was unfortunate enough to live right next to the rambunctious Cartwrights, described the noise as like 'murder' or somebody in 'a considerable amount of pain'. Another claimed that Caroline's screaming and shouting during the horizontal tango was completely drowning out the sound from their television. And an additional complainant made sure that everyone knew Steve was in on the whole thing too: '[One night] I heard a male voice howling loudly,' Marjorie Hall told the court, 'which I felt was very unnerving.' Unnerving indeed, Marjorie!

Just in case the whole neighbourhood was playing a naughty joke on the Cartwrights, Sunderland County Council ordered that their house have specialist equipment left inside for a few days in order to register the levels of noise. It turned out that Steve and Caroline were regularly raising the noise level to 30 or 40 decibels, sometimes reaching 47.

Steve and Caroline, (who were not traditionally attractive by most standards) had somehow managed to also elicit complaints from the local postman – yes, seriously – and a woman who walked her young son to school past the Cartwright household, presumably who then had to endure half an hour of the most awkward conversation of her life. In my day, sex education was a graphic video of childbirth followed by a lecture about abstinence and years of trauma counselling. It was a more innocent age.

The Cartwrights claimed that when their neighbours brought up their noisy sessions, they made a genuine effort to keep it down. Caroline said that she'd even tried sex with a pillow over her face to keep herself from screaming out, but then she 'started to cry'. Having listened to a ten-minute-long recording of the Cartwrights' 'hysterical' sexual liaisons, however, a judge wasn't amused. He agreed that such activity was loud enough to be genuinely disturbing to most people on the street. This husband and wife sounded like they were hacking each other to death nightly.

Steve and Caroline had already been served with a noise abatement notice by the time they arrived in court to hear full testimonies from everyone on their street. This had attempted to ban them from 'shouting, screaming or vocalisation at such a level as to be a statutory nuisance', but it turned out that these kids just couldn't keep their hands off each other – or at least not in a way that didn't let the entire population of Sunderland know about it. Caroline was brought in to be convicted for breaching the notice, but had a surprising argument up her sleeve: she claimed that her 'right to respect for her private and family life', under Article 8 of the Human Rights Act, was being violated by the curtain-twitchers who couldn't stop talking about her sex life. When that failed to convince people, she also brought in a sexual psychologist to testify that she couldn't help making the noises. No, I couldn't believe that when I read it either!

THE VERDICT

The court handed them an ASBO which they breached after which they were given a suspended sentence. But do they really have a human right to do whatever they want in the bedroom if it's so obnoxiously loud that it makes neighbours lose sleep? Does it count in their favour if they tried solutions such as pillows over their faces to minimise the noise? And how many people really do manage to keep a straight face in an official legal arena while a ten-minute-long recording of two people having full-on screaming intercourse reverberates throughout the room? Learn what to do about a noisy neighbour at the end of the chapter.

SUPERSTAR NEIGHBOURS

Lastly, there's the question on all of our minds: what happens when, inevitably, a celebrity realises the sparkling appeal of your neighbourhood and moves in next door?

The Blairs

GQ editor Dylan Jones in 2007 was so moved by his own plight that he wrote a *Daily Mail* article about it.

When Cherie and Tony Blair moved close to him, they had really ruined his quiet little idyll, he argued, and he couldn't even work out exactly how they'd found it, being as it was 'tucked away behind Marble Arch' in the middle of central London. Now journalists were camping along the street, shopkeepers had signs in their windows saying 'WELCOME CHERIE', traffic cones lined the pathway and armed police in bulletproof vests were really interfering with the aesthetics of his walk to work.

The fact that Tony Blair is one of the top five living targets for a terrorist attack, Dylan said, hasn't escaped his notice. Poor Mr Jones now lives in a state of perpetual fear, giving a wide berth to the £3.5-million Georgian townhouse in case it is blown to smithereens any second. Paddington has become his personal Iraq.

And as if that all weren't bad enough, his neighbours roll their eyes in a really antisocial manner every time the blacked-out car with its reinforced glass makes it way along the mews. Building work that involves setting up a panic room, as well as advanced motion detectors, alarm systems and CCTV cameras, is now the norm, along with that unrelenting media circus outside. It must have escaped Dylan's notice that by writing about the problem as a journalist himself, he may well be adding to the whole thing. After all, the poor lamb has been driven nearly to distraction by hardship; no one could reasonably expect him to think straight.

We've probably all looked around our local area and thought: It's only a matter of time before a former prime minister moves here. Clearly it's not just editors of large-scale men's magazines who are at risk, but potentially the entire public – which is why Dylan took the time to warn us through the medium of print.

SO WHAT CAN I DO?

So what exactly can you do if someone comes along, buys up a house and turns your street into a building site? Can you blame them if their alarm systems and CCTV arrangements make everyone else feel uncomfortable? Does it count as unfair intrusion if a well-known person, or a person who decides that they are in some way at risk, puts up traffic cones or designates their own parking space right outside your house, when you had no such right? Do celebrities really have more rights to their neighbourhood than the non-famous residents around them?

- **Talk to each other!**
  Always try this first. BT were on to something with their slogan 'It's good to talk'. What wise words they are. Quite often people do not realise they are causing problems for others. The neighbours who leave their dog alone in the house during the day when they go to work may be unaware that the dog is howling in loneliness. The man who is using his latest all-singing-and-dancing profes-sional over-powered buzz saw, building an ark in the garden at 1am, may be oblivious to the pain he is causing to neighbours.

  The way forward may be to speak to the dog owners in the friendliest, most caring, concerned and supportive manner, asking if everything is all right with their beau-tiful animal because it constantly cries and howls during the day. You could drop into the conversation that you are a night worker and their darling labradoodle wakes you up in the process. In the second scenario it may be good to express an interest in the fine project being undertaken by the neighbour Noah, admiring his dedica-tion. Perhaps you could point out that you have checked the long-range weather forecast, that he has longer than he thinks to finish the project and 7 or 8pm would be a very thoughtful time to finish.

  In many cities – London especially – we tend not to know our neighbours so the first time we have anything to do with them is often when things have gone wrong. Do not get off on the wrong foot. A huge number of cases end up in court because one or other neighbour has written an ill-judged letter or email (or, worse, posted something on Facebook) rather than simply going next door and asking nicely for things to change.

- **Mediation**
  If talking to your neighbour doesn't work, then depending on the circumstances you could consider mediation: sometimes – whether you like it or not – there are two sides to a story! Most local authorities would be able to provide a free mediation service between yourself and your neighbour, where an independent person will speak with you both and try to negotiate a peaceful solution. Again, however, this does not always work.

- **Abatement orders**
  Noise and nuisance are problems that need fixing. You can complain in person, by telephone or by email to the environmental health department of your local authority. If the neighbour's behaviour is damaging to your health or a nuisance, this is known as a statutory nuisance and is straightforward antisocial behaviour which you should report to the police.

  If you live in rented accommodation, you should also inform your landlord, local authority or housing association. They can offer additional support, which might include fitting locks, vandal-proof letterboxes, fences and lighting, and installing alarms which might even be linked to your local police station. If the offending neighbour lives in the same building as you, they can also confront them and warn them about possible tenancy agreement breaches, and the possibility of eviction.

  Local authorities have regulatory powers to help them

manage noise and nuisance, including the Environmental Protection Act 1990. The Act places a duty on them to take reasonable steps to investigate complaints from people living in its area about alleged statutory nuisance.

If the issue is a nuisance that is harmful to health (like Gordon's case) the local authority must serve an abatement notice on the person responsible. If the person doesn't comply with the notice they could be prosecuted.

If the council decides someone is causing a statutory noise nuisance they must issue a noise abatement order. The order may require that the noise be stopped altogether or limited to certain times of day or else they will face further legal action. The notice can be served on the person responsible for the noise, who then has 21 days to appeal.

- o **What exactly qualifies as a nuisance?**
    1. noise (including loud music and barking dogs)
    2. artificial light (except street lamps)
    3. dust, steam, smell or insects from business premises
    4. smoke, fumes or gases
    5. a build-up of rubbish that could harm health

If someone breaks an abatement order about noise from their home, they can be fined up to £5,000. If it's noise from a factory or business, the penalty can be up to £20,000.

- • **ASBOs**
Abatement orders do not always work. Even when breaches result in fines, their payment does not guarantee the end of the problem.

In very serious cases of antisocial behaviour, the police and local councils can work together to seek antisocial behaviour orders (ASBOs) against people aged 10 and over who are causing alarm, harassment and distress to others.

The purpose of the ASBO is to protect the public and should reduce the risk of further antisocial behaviour by stopping the offender from doing certain things, such as burning toxic material in bonfires, having over-loud marital relations, or playing Holst's *The Planets* too loudly in their garden at 3am. The terms of the order can vary depending on the antisocial behaviour that is complained of.

An ASBO can also be imposed by a magistrate or judge while sentencing someone for a criminal offence of an antisocial crime, and breaking or 'breaching' the ASBO is a criminal offence.

- **Criminal offences**
  - On occasion, the behaviour of a neighbour from hell becomes a straightforward criminal offence.
  - Shooting air rifles beyond house boundaries, from private premises into a public area, or within 50ft (15m) of the centre of any highway are offences under the Firearms Act 1968. If you think your neighbour has been moronically firing weapons you *must* get the police involved as soon as possible.
  - Be advised that evidence is required and this usually requires corroboration – certainly a bit more than one person saying someone did something and the other saying they didn't.
  - Keeping a diary of the antisocial behaviour, by as many affected neighbours as possible, and keeping a record of how the behaviour has negatively affected

your health, will assist the local authorities and police to deal with toxic neighbours.

- **Police involvement**
  - Always contact the police if you or others are at risk or in imminent danger. You should call the police if your neighbour:
    1. is violent, threatening or abusive
    2. is harassing you sexually, or because of your sexuality, religion or ethnic background
    3. is breaching the peace (being disorderly in the street or making a lot of noise)
    4. is breaking the law in any other way – or if you suspect this.

  - Although noise nuisance is generally treated as an environmental health matter, to be handled by the local council, the police can deal with a complaint if the noise amounts to a breach of the peace, or where it is associated with threatening, violent or other antisocial behaviour.
  - Always contact the police over incidents or behaviour that concerns you. It doesn't matter how many times you have to ring them; they will (or should) record your complaint and act upon it depending on its severity, but may just give advice. Most importantly, however, obtain the name of the police officer or staff member you are talking to and keep a record of this in your diary. It's amazing sometimes how this simple action jars someone from a fobbing-off action to one of correct procedure.

- **Taking your neighbour to court**
  - Taking someone to court yourself (as opposed to letting the authorities deal with your toxic neighbour) can be expensive, so it should be your last resort and is only an option if nothing else works. Publicly funded legal representation is not normally available for this type of action. However, under the Legal Help scheme you may be entitled to free or subsidised legal advice and help to prepare your case. Your local law centre, advice centre or Citizens Advice Bureau may be able to give you advice on your eligibility. Some charitable institutions may provide free advice and finance proceedings, but this is by no means a certainty. Solicitors very often provide free advice in introductory meetings.
  - A solicitor might be prepared to enter into a 'no win, no fee' agreement. The solicitor will not take any fees from you if the action fails but will be entitled to a fee plus a percentage increase if the case succeeds. If you lose the case, you may have to pay the other party's legal costs and other expenses.

- **What about the Blairs?**
  In determining whether your neighbour's conduct has been reasonable or not, the court will consider first and foremost whether their behaviour has been reasonable and proportional. Politicians (like the Blairs) and pop stars are, for example, entitled to take reasonable measures to protect their privacy, family and home within the law. We the public put them where they are and some nuisances, such as the paparazzi camping outside their homes, we just have to – within reason – put up with.

RINDER'S RULES

- Disputes can nearly always be avoided by speaking to your neighbours calmly and thoughtfully about any issue before getting the authorities involved. *Speak before you commence legal proceedings.*

- If you do have a genuine neighbour from hell, get in touch with your local council and – depending on the circumstances – the police.

- Keep a diary and any evidence in support of the complaint that you have against your neighbour.

- However much you can't stand them, always attempt to mediate before going to court (you can find relevant mediation services in the Appendix to this book).

CHAPTER 5

TERRIBLE
TRADESMEN

Although I am not especially religious I do believe that there is (or at least ought to be) a special place in hell for rogue builders (sadly the Lord has stopped responding to my customer service suggestions since I was expelled from Sunday school for asking too many awkward questions). Dodgy builders do not just ruin people's homes; they can – and often do – destroy people's lives. The financial and emotional relationship we have with our homes runs very deep, so when we hire someone to work in our sacred space and they fall short on delivering what they promised we can end up devastated. The good news is that if you find yourself in this sorry situation there are a number of legal weapons at your disposal; the bad news is that toxic workmen are as troubled by legal action as I am by moronic Twitter trolls (that is, not one bit).

I know you will enjoy the stories I have selected below and you will read the legal advice carefully. If you take nothing else away from this chapter, however, please remember this: before hiring a builder (or any workman) check, check and check again all their references. If you have any doubt about them at all, use someone else. And remember, they are probably offering to do the job 50 per cent cheaper for a reason!

CRIMINAL BUILDERS

The cautionary tale of the cowboy tradesman has lurked in our national consciousness for decades. In times long past, someone might have sold you a cat concealed in a sack and told you it was a goose ideal for Christmas; nowadays, someone will sell you a sheet of tarpaulin pulled over a couple of sticks and tell you it's a charming extension ideal for Great-Aunt Hilda. This problem is so common that it's estimated the average household loses £600 every year to incompetent tradesmen, while 17 per cent of people who have work done on their home will end up having to have it redone at a later date. So don't forget the moral of the fairytale: *if you don't want a wolf to blow your house down, then don't be a naive little pig.*

Unfortunately, you can't exactly plan for the rogue builder who smashes up your kitchen, or the plumber who tells you he's qualified to deal with leaks but fails to mention that the most training he's ever experienced in that area was when he changed his 1-year-old son's nappy. But you can read up on your rights before you ask a person you don't know to deal with your hot tub, and you might just find yourself saving a lot of money and hassle if you do.

Dodgy builder wanted: good price offered

In 2009 Mark Killick went to prison. He'd spent the last few years operating as a rogue builder, going into people's houses and doing (for thousands of pounds) what a bunch of 17-year-olds and a couple of bottles of vodka would have happily done for free. In other words, he would arrive, take some money up front, trash the place and skip off with the cash.

Having gotten away with this for a few years, Mark celebrated by buying himself a Porsche. Because after all that hard work defrauding grannies on the doorstep – some of them might have even questioned the time frames, and Lord knows that takes up valuable con-artist time – he thought he really deserved a shiny, sports-car-shaped pat on the back.

Everything had gone to plan for so long for Mark, but then one too many people complained and it all went spectacularly wrong in a very short amount of time. He got hauled up in front of a judge and ended up bankrupt and shamefaced in jail, on a big time-out that was intended to get him thinking about what he had done. When he came back out into society, supposedly a reformed character, he got thinking about what he could do with his life after the dizzying highs and the disappointing lows of living as an old-lady-baiting cowboy tradesman with a Porsche where his conscience should have been. He took a good, hard look at himself and at society, he racked his brains and he thought for at least five minutes about the reaches of his personal potential. And, eventually, he knew what he was going to do the second time around. He was going to be an old-lady-baiting cowboy tradesman with a Porsche where his conscience should have been.

What Mark lacked in imagination, he made up for in deviousness. Straight out of the clink, he changed his name from Killick to Jenkins, set himself up on a website for trusted tradesman, and registered three different companies – Pro-Fit Builders, XL Builders and Trade Bookers – with competitive prices to draw customers in. Most people who saw the names of these companies reasonably assumed that Mark was therefore in charge of a respectable group of tradesmen who knew the basics of building and engineering. The reality, of course, was that it was still just Mark, cruising the south-west on his own, with no discernible skill base, destroying houses right and left for personal gain.

Despite his time spent inside, Mark assumed that the worst that could happen next was merely the equivalent of some sympathetic cartoon lawyer listening to the victims' complaints, cocking his head and saying with a laugh: 'That Mark, eh? What's he like!' With this in mind, he skipped off to the bank with some more pocketed cash, paid it in and then promptly spent £62,000 of it gambling online. Altogether, he ended up accruing £1.4 million from his unwitting clients, who all thought they were going to get the dream conservatory they'd been saving up for four years, but instead got the construction equivalent of a slap in the face.

Of course, the victims of Mark's shoddy building work weren't stupid: they were just far too trusting. When he told them that work would take a lot longer than expected, they believed that was for the best. When he declared dodgy-looking electricals safe, they thought he knew what he was talking about. When he claimed that it was standard to ask for a £20,000 deposit at the beginning of a renovation, they fell for his charm and his confident way of claiming expertise. So, when he disappeared without a trace, or dragged out the work for another few weeks, or produced faulty sockets or kitchen tiles with plastic sheeting poking out from behind them, what were they supposed to do? Does the law have the ability to protect them, even after their houses have been irreparably damaged and the money has been paid? Can a persistent offender like Mark Killick-turned-Jenkins ever truly be brought to justice?

THE VERDICT

The saddest thing about Mark Jenkins's criminality is that the consequences for his 42 victims were so far-reaching. A lot of couples testified in court against him, claiming that they had almost divorced because of the strain after their houses were nearly ruined and their hard-earned savings were taken (if you think watching your husband attempt DIY is stressful, try watching him hire someone to do it). Some had suffered financially for ten years or more because of the hideous mistakes Jenkins had made. One particularly harrowing tale came from a man who had wanted to move his dying grandmother into his house for her final days, promising her that she wouldn't have to die in hospital. Jenkins stretched out the building work indefinitely, which led to the poor grandmother passing away in the place she had never wanted to, hours after uttering her final words: 'When can I come home?' A truly distressing tale of a caring family taken to task by a heartless conman.

So what did become of Mark in the end? Well, like all good stories, this one involves a bad guy's comeuppance: he was jailed for five years and publicly shamed across the media (again) in 2014. No prizes, however, for guessing which career he decides upon when he leaves prison for the second time.

SO WHAT CAN I DO?

Sometimes, a tradesman ruining your day is all relative: Prince Charles famously railed against his gardeners when the azaleas they planted around his Highgate estate bloomed bright orange instead of tranquil pink, for instance, and had the unfortunate workers dig them all up and replace them with the colour scheme he preferred. The horrors that he's had to live through truly know no bounds, do they? When you hear tales of monarchical torment like that, you begin to realise Anne Boleyn got off lightly.

Perhaps the gardeners in question, then, should have known that the Prince preferred pink, but most people wouldn't have a legal leg to stand on if they held a workman to account for offending their sensibilities with the garishness of the flowers they planted. If your story is a little less 'Prince Charles and the azaleas' and a little more 'Mark Jenkins the millionaire gambling addict and the ruined lives of 42 homeowners', then rest assured that you probably will have some courtroom recourse available to you. You just need to know where to start.

Has a crime been committed?

Mark Killick was quite rightly convicted and imprisoned for his crimes. Once investigations commenced it was clear that he had deliberately set out to take people's money with no intention of completing any of the work he was supposed to do.

In his case there appears to be a wealth of evidence that his intentions from the start were dishonestly to obtain money by doing very little, if any, work of any acceptable standard. He changed his name; he set up three companies to allow him to widen his web of victims; he had the talk; he had huge amounts of trusting, honest people's money.

Bogus, bandit, rogue, cowboy builders – call them what you will – often commit criminal offences. They can be experienced, even qualified, builders but with little or no work ethic and certainly no honesty. They know what they are doing but ramp up the problems: getting the homeowner to pay for unneeded expensive parts; installing inferior parts but charging for more expensive products; actually damaging householders' property so that the items have to be replaced; claiming for work they have not done, or inflating the time they spent on a job.

They are often unqualified but manage to persuade customers that they could build the Pyramids in two weeks and would be free to start next Monday if a deposit could be made as soon as possible. They regularly claim falsely to belong to trade associations or have qualifications that are completely bogus. Many of them have some building experience, but when they do not know what to do they get by, wing it, fly by the seat of their pants, and hope for the best. This is usually to the detriment of the customer and sometimes so disastrous as to leave the place in an extremely dangerous condition and requiring the owner to start again.

Many of those I have just described could be prosecuted for fraud by false representation, or by failing to disclose information, facing terms of imprisonment of up to ten years. In simple terms fraud is committed by a dishonest person getting something from you by telling lies.

Although some of the builders may have committed crimes, this is not always so easy to prove. Prosecution is not necessarily a given. If a builder says that he is registered as a gas–safe engineer (the Gas Safe Register replaced CORGI in 2009–10) when he is not, the householder would almost certainly not have proceeded with the work if they had known the truth. Apart from the obvious danger, any damage caused as a result of the unqualified person's work would in all likelihood not be insured. However, does every householder ask if the builder is so qualified? The genuine gas fitter will produce his Gas Safe Register ID card and allow you to record his seven-digit licence number. Did the builder produce a business card or invoice claiming that he was registered? One person's word against another's is not as good evidence at court as paper.

If a plumber informs you that your water pump has broken, can you prove otherwise? It is more difficult, if not impossible, to prove it wasn't broken before our cowboy got his hands on it. Both instances would be suitable for fraud charges to be made if the evidence was available.

If you believe you are the victim of crime by a rogue builder, inform the police. Complain to Trading Standards, which takes a very harsh view of rogue traders.

It is not just our homes

Surrey Council were becoming a little bit suspicious about what the tradesmen in the area were getting up to during work. They had that nagging feeling we all know well: the suspicion that the builders, plumbers, boiler fitters, washing-machine repairers, drainage specialists and aerial technicians hired by the good people of Surrey might not be completely up to scratch. So what was to be done? Well, the council workers got in contact with a team of Trading Standards officers, and they decided not to overreact. They'd just set up a high-tech control room in a secret location, create a number of different building sites that needed various repairs, hire 44 randomly chosen tradesman from the borough, plant a few CCTV cameras, train a thespian-minded officer to pose as a vulnerable homeowner in the sting, then sit back and watch what happened over a number of weeks. Simple.

Now, you might be forgiven for reading the Mark Killick story and thinking that he was just one bad egg in a largely good batch. But what the Trading Standards officers found in Surrey confirmed that the council had been paranoid about the entire profession for a reason. On one particularly upsetting morning, they witnessed a plumber turning up to fix a water tank who promptly unzipped his trousers and urinated directly into it. Plumbing the depths of depravity, perhaps, but not doing any effective plumbing work elsewhere.

If that weren't bad enough, a repairman hired in the afternoon to fix a leak in a gas tank was caught on camera trying to find the leak by using a lighter – as if he could afford to lose any more IQ points in the gas explosion that would have happened if the council hadn't made up the leak in the first place.

Later on, traders turned up claiming to be members of organisations that they weren't, spouting off about experience they didn't have, charging four times the going rate for small repairs, and taking five hours to complete contracted work that should only have taken one. At the more surreal end of the scale, one supposed drain specialist turned up to deal with a blockage in a fancy-dress outfit rather than anything resembling protective clothing. The council's final report was unclear about exactly which fancy-dress outfit the man wore to unclog the pipes, but I like to imagine it was Scar from *The Lion King*.

'If you didn't have the film evidence, you wouldn't actually believe what you were seeing,' one of the officers involved in the operation told the BBC after it had finished. Ten of the tradesmen involved were criminally prosecuted, so underhanded were their techniques. Additionally, five were told that they would 'receive advice', and not in the cup-of-tea-and-a-biscuit, hand-on-the-shoulder, did-you-get-it-wrong-because-you're-having-a-tough-time-outside-of-work way. All in all, the council and Trading Standards estimated that one in four workers hired carried out repairs that were either substandard or outright dangerous. Many of them strung out their hours for extra pay on top of that.

After the BBC reported on the Surrey Council findings, stories poured in from people elsewhere. One particularly memorable one came from an Englishman living in the Netherlands, who claimed that builders there had managed to fit a Jacuzzi in his bathroom that leaked directly into the electrical mains. The builder who made this potentially catastrophic error was let off in the Dutch courts, with the judge claiming that 'these things happen', presumably before taking another drag on his legalised cannabis and wandering off to call some artwork 'groovy'.

SO WHAT CAN I DO?

So what can you do if the person who's supposed to repair your problem seems to have done the opposite? Is the judge more likely to side with you, or to act as though construction gone wrong is more unlucky than malicious? How can you verify if a workman claiming to be a member of a trusted trading organisation like the UK Gas Safety Register actually isn't lying through his teeth? And what's the best way of going about finding someone who doesn't reduce your hopes of a properly functioning drainage system to a pipe dream?

Criminal prosecutions can be pursued but the damage has usually been done by then and convictions do not compensate for the heartache, anguish and financial loss often associated with those cases. It is obviously better to avoid getting caught out by a rogue builder in the first place.

Finding your builder

- In the first instance, be sure you know what it is you want built or fixed. You do not want to be persuaded to build a new conservatory when all you needed was a leaky roof repaired.

• Ask friends and neighbours if they could recommend a good builder. They cannot guarantee the work but their satisfaction is worth a lot. Local building, plumbing and electrical suppliers can be a way of finding decent tradesmen or -women. Local suppliers know established builders and are unlikely to recommend a builder that would let them down.

• The internet can be a good source and the builder's website will usually contain the details of trade associations or professional bodies they profess to belong to (see list in the Appendix). A search of the company name may throw up positive or negative comments from past customers. There are sites which have reviews of builders, but while they can be helpful, remember you never know who wrote a review. It could be the builder bigging themselves up or a disgruntled ex-partner wishing a lifetime of unemployment on their former beloved.

• Check builders' business cards and invoices for addresses. Only consider those with an address or you may have trouble finding them later. Too many tradesmen only have a mobile-phone number. If you look carefully at their white vans you will often see a magnetic removable trade sign with the company name, what they do and a phone number. No address is a clear warning sign.

• Check whether they belong to a professional body or a trade association. Be quite open about taking the details and membership numbers from them; make enquiries with the associations. The associations and regulatory bodies welcome these requests.

- Ask the builder for the details of similar recent projects they have finished so that you can make enquiries. Genuine builders will not have any issue with supplying these references (but allow the builder time to speak to their previous customer to ensure they are OK with you contacting them).

- You can find out whether a builder is solvent with a simple credit check. It will take about a minute and will cost around £6.

Once I have chosen my builder, what do I do next?

- Obtain a written signed quote on headed business paper, covering all the work to be done, materials to be used and cost including VAT. Beware of builders who advise you to save money by not paying the VAT and giving them cash.

- Get more than one quote and beware of quotes that are ridiculously cheaper than others; it may be a sign the builder does not have a clue as to what is involved.

- Ask to see the builder's insurance certificate and take a copy; bandits do not usually bother with such inconveniences. If you get a quote from a builder they cannot charge more than it says, even if the agreed work ends up costing them more than they thought. Ensure that there is a written signed contract setting out what work is to be done, what materials are to be used and the cost including VAT. If they won't give you a written quote or contract, it could mean that they plan to charge in excess of what was originally agreed, or claim that they never agreed to do certain work. *A contract is vital and without it your legal position is weak.*

- If the builder asks for payment up front to cover the cost of materials, they may be unreliable. An honest builder with a successful business should be able to afford the building materials and recover the costs when the work is finished. However, use your judgement; you may decide that, in these austere times, drip-feeding small amounts against receipt (and never in cash) may be reasonable.

- Be cautious about builders who want to start immediately. Some bandits will sign up to do a lot of work in a particular area, start the jobs or complete them to a poor standard, then go somewhere else, with a new company name and new telephone number to avoid being traced by their victims. Of course, you may have just hit on a timely window of opportunity with your builder, a few weeks clear in their diary because of a cancellation. Again use your own judgement to assess the situation.

- Take the registration numbers of the different cars used by the builders. Take note of the names of those employed on the site. Take a photograph of the builders if you can surreptitiously do this. This is all good evidence if it goes wrong and the police want to trace them. You may feel like you are being silly, but you'll be the silly one when you are left with dodgy work and no way to track down the guys who did it.

- Keep a diary of the progress of the project.

- Photograph key stages.

What happens when you realise things are going wrong?

- Once you have taken the plunge and the builder has started work, there may come a stage when alarm bells start ringing. The builder does not turn up every day, and when (and if) they answer the telephone there are excuses galore: 'Materials haven't arrived; the van's broken down; the weather is too bad.' It may be that the work is progressing but not as you required, or in such an unsatisfactory manner that you are getting very concerned. Photograph what the builder has done and keep a record of phone calls (even those that are never picked up), conversations with the builder, what agreements you have made, when the builder turns up and what they have done.

- You should point out to the builder that they are employed to do your work in the time agreed. You may have included a clause in the contract setting out the deadline for the builder to complete it; otherwise they will legally be expected to do so in a 'reasonable time'.

- Where the work is not satisfactory, you should indicate what is wrong and give the builder an opportunity to bring the work up to standard and finish the job to the agreed specifications. If you have had plans or drawings prepared, use these to point out areas that have not been complied with or where agreed materials have not been used. You can set reasonable deadlines, making sure you use the phrase 'time is of the essence' verbally, but confirmed in writing, for the work to be completed.

- It is a legal obligation for builders to use materials that are supplied by them, of satisfactory quality, and fit for purpose. 'Of satisfactory quality' means that the materials need to be well made and in good condition. 'Fit for purpose' means that the materials are suitable for what they are being used for.

- The remedial work should be at the builder's expense. If they comply with your wishes, to your satisfaction, all is well except for the inconvenience you suffered due to delays and having to chivvy up a lazy, sloppy builder. In short it is important that you give the workman the opportunity to rectify errors.

What if the work is still not up to standard?

- If the builder has been given the opportunity to rectify what was wrong and it is still wrong, or the work is of such poor quality that you do not believe the builder can bring it up to standard, it may be advisable to get a second or third opinion from other reputable builders.

If their opinions are also that the work is bad and has not been done with reasonable care and skill, as required by the Supply of Goods and Services Act 1982, you can refuse to let the original builder continue with the work. The builder will have failed to meet the required standards and therefore failed to comply with their contractual obligations.

- You can demand a refund for the unsatisfactory work and claim for additional costs that you may have had to pay to get another builder to remedy their bad or shoddy service. If they refuse to pay, you can take them to court to claim the money back. It could be, however, that the cowboy is on his horse riding into the sunset, blissfully ignoring your pleas for refunds.

- At this stage, or even earlier, you should consider legal advice. You may be covered under your home insurance or you may have to pay. It is very unlikely that free legal aid of any type will be available.

- If you paid the builder with a credit card, you may be able to reclaim your money from the credit-card company under Section 75 of the Consumer Credit Act 1974.

- If the builder is genuinely a member of a trade association there may be a dispute-resolution scheme that you could use. Good trade associations will offer help if things go wrong.

- If the builder has insurance, you could try to make a claim on his insurance policy.

- If you're struggling to get your money back, contact Citizens Advice Bureau for help.

- If it is a case where criminal charges are unlikely and the police will not be involved, it can be a lot more difficult tracing the builder. If you have taken vehicle registration numbers you can for a fee obtain from the DVLC the address that the vehicle is registered to, but do not hold your breath that this is where you will find your builder. A Companies House check will give the registered address of the company if it is registered.

- If you can track down the cowboy builder and he refuses to refund your money, take him to court. If the total costs are less than £10,000, a small claims court is appropriate; you do not need a solicitor, it will not cost too much, and courts – like mine – will be incredibly sympathetic to you.

- Larger claims will require legal representation, leading to legal and court fees. There is no guarantee of success, and failure could mean paying the builder's legal fees. But be brave in any event!

- Finally, let me say now that there are thousands of good, honest, professional tradesmen throughout the country who abhor cowboys as much as we do. Often, even unqualified builders can produce the goods and do a good job. Provided that the householder has been made no false promises about their qualifications or ability, and they do what is required (so long as the workman doesn't touch electrics or gas fittings), then good luck to all concerned.

WHAT HAPPENS IF A PERSON YOU HAVE HIRED IS INJURED ON YOUR PROPERTY?

Nadia and Tomasz

Nadia Isaacs was a woman who knew what she wanted. She was so attached to order and tidiness in her house, in fact, that the judge in her eventual court case even took the time to describe her as 'a person of exacting standards' (a woman after my own heart)! She knew where she wanted her antiques, and she knew in what order she wanted the Christmas cards above her fireplace at her perfectly coordinated home in Hampstead. It seems she was the sort of mother who makes you dry yourself off with a frayed piece of rag after showering because the fluffy towels are reserved for 'posh guests' who never actually visit. And after she put white carpets down, nobody but *nobody* was ever going to step on them with anything less than a thorough hosing-down with disinfectant at the front door. That meant that the carpenter working on her roof repairs was definitely out. Even if access to the roof was through the house and over the carpets in question.

When Tomasz Kmiecic complained that the only safe way he could see to the roof was through her son's bedroom, Nadia was having none of it. They had a short altercation at the door, which culminated in Nadia pulling off an equally dramatic version of Gandalf's 'You shall not pass!' moment, and Tomasz had to accept that he was not getting through. Decidedly less precious about human life than she was about home upholstery (and who isn't that cynically inclined these days?), she handed him a ladder. 'Up you go, then, Tomasz,' I can imagine her saying. 'You'll be just fine.' Probably. I'm at least 50 per cent sure of it.

Although, of course, Tomasz wasn't just fine. Predictably, he fell off the ladder, shattering his right elbow and substantially injuring his hip and thigh. His lawyers claimed that he would never be able to work as a repairman again. So how far exactly can you go with controlling access to repair workers in your house? Do you owe them a pathway across your brand-new carpets through your son's bedroom, even if you are a 'person of exacting standards'? Is it OK to go as far as Nadia? Or is she accountable for what happened to poor Tomasz, especially considering that the accident may well have affected the rest of his career?

In this case, judges ruled in favour of the homeowner when Tomasz sued. At first, he was given the right to appeal in order to clarify the effects of European laws in the UK – but the Appeal Court also ruled in Nadia's favour. She didn't have to give him access to the easiest route, they ruled, when it was possible for him to construct another one. In fact, the people who were at fault were Tomasz's employers, a firm called Armag Decoration who contracted him for around £70 a day and didn't have insurance. It was because of their lack of insurance that Tomasz then attempted to sue Nadia for lost earnings.

WHAT IS THE LAW?

- Nadia and Tomasz's tale really centres on what duty of care a householder has to visitors, whether in a private capacity, as a friend, or in Tomasz's case as a contracted builder.

- Legally, a person who occupies land or other property (this includes you, whether you are the homeowner or a tenant) can be held liable for injury to a person who is on the premises. This is known as 'occupier's liability'.

- An occupier's duty of care is supported by a statute called the Occupiers' Liability Act 1957, which provides that an occupier has a duty 'to take such care as in all the circumstances of the case is reasonable to see that the visitor will be reasonably safe in using the premises for the purposes for which he is invited or permitted by the occupier to be there'.

- This liability extends to fixed or movable structures, which can include such things as chairs, ladders, scaffolding and lifts.

- The Act states that when a person is in the exercise of their trade, that person will not only appreciate the special risks associated with their trade but will also guard against them. This means that the occupier will be free to leave the tradesman to do just that and will not have a higher duty of care placed upon them. Most of the time, therefore, you do not need special insurance for workmen.

- The Act does, however, require an occupier to guard against hazards that might be of particular concern for workers coming on to the premises. Plumbers and electricians, for example, often need to go into lofts or other awkward places as part of their work. In those cases, the occupier will have a duty to take measures to ensure those areas are safe for the workmen.

- If a risk is willingly accepted by the visitor then the occupier will not be liable for any damage suffered. Signs such as 'Enter at your own risk' are good examples of this.

- One of the precautions the occupier might take to prevent a builder from encountering a hazard would be to give a warning, for example, that the earth in the back garden is particularly boggy and may not support a ladder safely.

And finally, a man and his handyman

Finally, there's an interesting tale that throws up the question of how much a man can truly love his electrician. In February 2015 this unusual case came about when an old man and his wife went to court to try and prove that they legally owned some very contentious works of art. These weren't your average prints from the local gallery, either – these were real, bona fide pieces from Picasso.

Pierre Le Guennec and his wife Danielle were in their twilight years, and starting to think about what their children might inherit when they inevitably passed away. Pierre, it turned out, had worked as an electrician and general handyman at Picasso's estate while the artist was still alive. Apparently, either Picasso or his wife (the couple disagreed on who it was, which doesn't exactly strengthen their case) boxed up a few of their less beloved artworks while clearing up a studio in the 1970s and handed them over to Pierre, saying, 'Here, this is for you. Take it home.'

Suspiciously, Pierre had then taken the pieces home without question and hidden them in his garage – rather than, say, proudly hanging them around his house, which I might humbly suggest one would consider doing with a Picasso if one owned a few – right up until the present day. But once he'd had them for so long, he realised that his kiddies might be implicated in a possible legal scandal and contacted the Picasso administration in the hopes that they would give everything a big thumbs-up. Unfortunately, not everything went to plan: the police confiscated the art, and Pierre and Danielle were ordered to court, accused of concealing stolen goods and facing the possibility of prison time and an extremely hefty fine.

So did Picasso have such an affinity with his handyman that he gave away a box of his works to him? It's possible, but hard to prove, because most of the key witnesses – including, obviously, Picasso himself – have died in the interim. And what happens if you suspect, or you know, that one of your own hired tradesmen has wandered off with a family heirloom, Picasso or no? How can you make sure that someone is held to account if they take a little memento of their time at your house away with them at the end of the job?

SO WHAT CAN I DO?

Prevention is the best cure. Remove temptation and minimise the risk of theft. In effect you are allowing strangers, people you do not know, even if they have a nice smile and splendid muscles, into your home. Take basic precautions.

- Lock up parts of the premises the workmen do not need access to, including bedrooms, sheds or the garage.

- Remove items of value such as jewellery, credit cards, mobile phones, chargers, computers, tablets, e-book readers, cameras and cash to a locked room or a safe if you have one.

- Keep photographs of jewellery and serial numbers of items to assist with identification if goods that are stolen are later recovered.

- Try not to leave workmen alone in your home.

- Do not give them keys to your house if you can avoid it. If you do, be prepared to change the locks when they have gone, or you may have unwanted visitors in the future. Your insurance company may not be too happy that you let house keys out of your possession when you are claiming for what was taken in a burglary.

- Remove sources of personal data (bank statements, bills, address books) from where they can be seen. Personal data is valuable to fraudsters.

- Tell the workmen from the start what parts of the building they can access and when. It is likely they will want to use your bathroom so ensure there are no knick-knacks there that will tempt them. Denying access to bathroom facilities could, as we know, result in one of them using your water tank.

- Check the premises every day when the workmen finish.

- Ensure the workman understands that only agreed building debris is to be removed. You may want to keep the Belfast sink that has been replaced, the copper water tank, or the 50kg of lead piping.

- If something is missing you need to be certain it was there when the workmen were present, that it could not have been moved innocently to another part of the house, and most importantly that one of the workmen took it.

- Theft is a serious allegation and difficult to prove. If there is only one person working in your home, early reporting to the police could result in the police acting expeditiously, searching the workman, his home and his vehicle, but the police would need convincing that an identifiable item was in all likelihood taken by the workman and that it was improbable anyone else could have nabbed it. When more than one workman is involved (unless something very valuable has gone missing) the police are unlikely to be able to obtain the required legal permission to search the home of each and every one of them.

RINDER'S RULES

- It is entirely irrelevant that your workman 'seems trustworthy'. Do not be a moron! Check all references thoroughly.

- Make sure that you have a clear contract setting out

exactly what is to be done, what materials are to be used, and how long the work is going to take to complete.

- Check the contract carefully and be rigid about enforcing it.

- Unless you are absolutely confident that the money is being used for your build *do not give any money up front*.

- Check the work carefully every day.

- In the event that you end up in some kind of dispute, seek to deal with the matter diplomatically. There is no point shouting at first. It will get you nowhere.

- Take regular photos and keep lists of the work that has been completed.

- If things go wrong and you are unsatisfied you must give the workman the chance to repair the work before slinging them out.

- If you are still unhappy, write to the builder formally demanding your money back and the cost of any repairs to the shoddy work they have carried out.

- In the event that the he/she doesn't respond or (worse still) has disappeared, seek legal advice if the amount you have spent is over £10,000; otherwise take the builder to the small claims court yourself where you are likely to appear before a sympathetic judge . . . like me!

NB: for relevant advice on how to issue proceedings against your builder and the details of trade assocations and other professional bodies mentioned in this chapter, please see the appendix.

CUSTODY BATTLES

Nothing makes me more cross than warring couples who use their children as weapons in their divorce proceedings. Whether I'm listening to a case involving a deadbeat father refusing to take financial responsibility for his children or a mother preventing Dad from having reasonable access to his children, I have – on more than one occasion – beckoned my court usher Michelle over to remove the gavel from my table as I have found the urge to throw it at one of litigants increasingly hard to resist. I do not care whether you cannot stand the sight of your ex, neither does it matter to me what he or she did to you emotionally. It is often wholly irrelevant. It is the duty of all parents to cast aside whatever anger they harbour against their ex-partner and place the interests of their children first. In other words, to act like grown-ups! Although the majority of parents do act responsibly, many do not and our family courts are – very sadly – clogged up with cases which could and should have been resolved way before they ended up in court.

This chapter deals with a number of issues involving custody battles over children. It is not an absolute account of what to do in the event you have a dispute; there are plenty of books on the subject and plenty of lawyers who can advise you (for a fee). Rather, this chapter should simply be used as a guide to what to do and, above all, how to behave, in the event that you end up in the tragic situation of dealing with a case involving the most important thing in your life: your child!

AN ACRIMONIOUS DIVORCE

The Baldwins

Of all the celebrity custody battles that have been mercilessly played out in the media, the one between Alec Baldwin and his wife Kim Basinger has to be one of the worst. Alec and Kim were both used to the high life, both successful in their acting careers, and both shared a complete lack of taste in baby names. They had a baby girl, named her Ireland, and should have settled down into familial loveliness right then. Unfortunately, it was very soon all going to end in tears.

To cut a long story short: Kim and Alec had their differences, and decided to divorce. The assets were split and the finances were sorted, but once negotiations started regarding little Ireland, these kitties showed pretty quickly that they both had claws. This was a custody battle that would end up dragging on for over three years.

Originally, Kim – who was living in LA, hours of flying time away from Alec's pad in New York – was given primary custody of Ireland, with Alec allowed visitation rights. This was in 2000. The battle commenced, and eventually Alec was awarded joint custody rights, flying back and forth across America to see his daughter with remarkable dedication. Part of this unusual agreement, which most non-millionaires would struggle to maintain, included Ireland having scheduled phone calls with her father at certain times.

Unwisely, Alec decided that the best time to schedule in a phone call with a pre-teen was 7.30 in the morning, a time when most 11-year-olds are about as responsive and prone to intellectual conversation as an afternoon tea with Paris Hilton. One fateful day in 2007, he learned this lesson the hard way. He picked up his mobile phone in New York, dialled the number, and waited for his little ray of sunshine to pick up. The long dial tone rang. And it rang. And it rang. And then it hit voicemail.

Now, plenty of parents are incensed by their 11-year-old child's lack of motivation to get out from under the bedcovers, but Alec decided to take it to a whole new level. He was going to do something about this. Hell, he was going to give her *a piece of his mind*. And so he did, via a particularly mad-sounding rant that predictably made its way onto the US entertainment site TMZ about five seconds after he left it.

'You are a rude, thoughtless little pig,' he told his daughter, presumably all the while still believing that this was A Really Good Idea. 'You don't have the brains or the decency as a human being. I don't give a damn that you're 12 years old, or 11 years old, or that you're a child, or that your mother is a thoughtless pain in the ass who doesn't care about what you do as far as I'm concerned.' The message went on from there, but I think we've all learned what we need to know from that snippet.

Needless to say, Alec got a metaphorical smack in the face for himself after leaving that voicemail in a moment of extremely bad judgement: he lost all previous custody rights to his daughter, and was barred from seeing her entirely. The judge ruled that he had proven himself unfit to spend time with Ireland if a missed phone call on an April morning was enough to send him swearing incoherently. It was a monumentally bad call, not much improved by him making further comments about Kim in the media and claiming that 'parental alienation' on her part had driven him to it. Not the most remorseful of reactions.

The good news is that this story eventually has a happy ending: Alec pulled himself together after a while, made a public apology and now has a fully functional relationship with his daughter. In the end, it serves to show who really suffers the most in a nasty custody battle: the child. But luckily, Ireland Baldwin grew up to be a fashion model towering over her parents at 6ft 2in – so if Alec tries to openly call her a swine again, it must be reassuring for her to know that she can comfortably take him down with a flick of her expensive high heels.

THE VERDICT

The case of Alec, Kim and Ireland throws up a number of questions. Firstly, how exactly is child custody decided in the first place? Can it really be swiped away if someone is found to have left their little girl a particularly shirty voicemail – or, in David Hasselhoff's memorable case, after being filmed drunkenly eating a cheeseburger off a hotel-room floor in Las Vegas? Why exactly would anyone worth millions of dollars not just order a new burger in the first place? And is it possible for one parent with a good legal team to cook up a story about the other – say, systematic 'parental alienation' – and have them declared unfit to look after a child because of it?

SO WHAT CAN I DO?

- It goes without saying that in law, all parents have a legal responsibility to support their children.

- In the UK, mothers automatically have parental responsibility for their children. Fathers have this right if they were married to the mother when the child was born.

- An unmarried father has parental responsibility if his name is registered on the child's birth certificate. The mother can consent to the father's name being added to the birth certificate, but if this consent is not forthcoming the father will have to apply for a court order to get parental responsibility. This is often the basis of serious dispute.

- It is in the child's interests that important issues as to how the child is raised are discussed by its parents: where the child will live and with which parent; holidays; what contact is acceptable; how the child will be supported financially; the religion if any the child is to be raised in; how the child is to be exposed to hereditary culture, and how the child is to be educated. YOU SHOULD DO EVERYTHING POSSIBLE TO ATTEMPT TO REACH AGREEMENT ON THIS.

- It is usually only when such agreement cannot be reached that a legal remedy, through a Family Panel or a Family Court, may be necessary.

- The most important legislation used in family courts covering children's interests is the Children Act 1989. If the court needs to determine a question relating to a child's upbringing, the court will always put the best interests of the child first. Children, if they are old enough to understand what is going on around them, are allowed and encouraged to contribute to decisions made about them, and to be kept informed about what is happening.

- Where contact or residence cannot be agreed it is usually sensible for the parents to consult a solicitor who specialises in family law, who will advise on how best to proceed. If you can't afford one, you *may* be entitled to legal aid but only if the case is particularly complicated.

- Before any proceedings can be brought before a judge parents are required to attend a mediation information assessment meeting where an impartial, trained mediator assists them to resolve or make progress with their disputes. This is, obviously, not applicable in domestic violence cases.

- Depending on personal circumstances the mediation meeting must be paid for. But it may be possible to get help with the cost (www.gov.uk/legal-aid). The nearest family mediation service can be found by visiting the government's website gov.uk, under 'family mediation'.

- Parents may need to go to court to obtain a Child Arrangements Order if mediation doesn't work.

A Child Arrangements Order determines:
1. where the child will live
2. when and what time the child spends with each parent
3. when and what other types of contact, like phone calls, take place

- Parents can also make applications without legal assistance by downloading the application form (C100) at gov.uk.

- Child Arrangements Orders replace what were previously called 'residence orders' and 'contact orders'. Currently a £215 fee is payable to the court when an order is applied for but depending on financial circumstances parents may be eligible for a reduced fee or they may not have to pay. A booklet EX160A 'Court and Tribunal Fees – Do I have to pay them?' is available from any court office or through the website hmctsformfinder. justice.gov.uk

- Parents appearing before the Family Court will be asked to explain their reasons for wanting access or residency, and in the latter case why residency should be granted to a particular parent. They are likely to be asked how they would cope, what financial arrangements are in place, and what environment the child will be raised in. If there are issues that would impact on the court's decision as to who should look after the child, such as domestic violence, substance abuse or alcoholism, these will obviously be taken into consideration before decisions are made.

- A court welfare officer will be appointed to assess the parents' home environment and how they interact with and look after the children. They will submit a report, including recommendations, to the family panel. Children who are old enough to understand what is going on will have the benefit of speaking to the court welfare officer.

- At the hearing, the magistrate(s) will try to establish:
  1. what the parents can agree
  2. what they can't agree
  3. if the child is at risk in any way

- Agreement, if it's in the child's best interests and if there are no concerns about the child's welfare, can end the process. The court will make a consent order which sets out what is agreed, if necessary.

- If agreement cannot be reached at the first court hearing the judge or magistrate will set a timetable for what happens next and the parents may be asked to try again to reach an agreement, e.g. by going to a meeting with a mediator.

- Parents may have to go on a Separated Parents Information Programme course if their case is about contact issues.

- The decision of the Family Court is legal and binding. It will be based on the following:
  1. your child's wishes and feelings
  2. your child's physical, emotional and educational needs
  3. the effect any changes may have on your child

4. your child's age, gender, characteristics and background
5. any possible risk of harm to your child
6. your ability to meet your child's needs

- Where residency has been given to one parent the court will normally settle on visiting rights. It will be agreed how often and for how long you see your children each day or each week. The court may also rule that telephone calls are allowed in between visits in order to maintain some level of continuity between parents. Just don't leave any Baldwin-esque answerphone messages!

RINDER'S RULES

- Do everything possible to avoid going to court. If you end up in a courtroom, there is a good chance that one (or both of you) has failed your children. Other than in the most serious circumstances you should be able to resolve things through mediation.

- Remember that whether or not your ex is a complete moron, he or she is still your child's parent! Never poison your kids against their father or mother. If your previous partner was an irretrievable fool, there is a good chance that your children will discover this on their own without your help!

- When you get your court order, you are *not* entitled to stop paying for your child even if your ex is refusing to live up to their side of the bargain and give you custody. It is not a bargain. You must do exactly as *you* have agreed! I hear far too many cases where (usually but not exclusively) Dad says, 'I stopped paying because she won't let me see them!' The bottom line is that you *cannot* do this. Ever! You must continue to live up to any agreement you have made regardless of what your partner does. In the event that your ex continues to disobey a court order, I can assure you that a judge will have no sympathy whatsoever. Watch my court if you have any doubt about this!

PARENTAL CASES OF CHILD ABDUCTION

So what happens if parents who divorce are not only emotionally estranged but also separated by a considerable distance? What happens when two courts on opposite sides of the world start trying to decide on the same case, the same child and the same family in very different ways? Read on for a dramatic story of parental child abduction.

Molly's case

In 2006 Molly Campbell was taken to Pakistan by her father. She was 12 years old, she'd last been seen at the school gates, and her mother was determined that she had been abducted.

As eager paparazzi hungry for a splash descended upon the family, it became completely unclear what the real story was. Molly appeared at a press conference in Lahore, claiming that her name was Misbah Rana and that she had fled a 'living hell' with her mother in her native Scotland. She said that she wanted to live with her father – but her mother said that she'd been taken away by force. The tabloids were insistent that she had been put on a flight to Pakistan with an arranged marriage in mind.

The truth of the matter begins in Glasgow in the 1980s. Louise Robinson met her boyfriend Sajad Rana round the local estate, walking her dogs, and the two were smitten with each other. He was a lovable tearaway from his conservative Muslim family; she was from a broken home, living with a stepdad who eventually bagged up her belongings and threw them out of the window. Both of them were looking for happiness and security with someone a little different from the other people they knew. They found that in each other.

So Sajad and Louise got married, had four children together, and decided to raise them together as Muslims. Louise wanted to embrace the family and culture of her husband, having very little contact with the family from her own troubled and unstable background. She wore traditional Islamic clothes, learned the Urdu language, and gave her children Pakistani names: Omar, Adam, Tahmina, and the youngest, Misbah.

Misbah was always known by both her official name and a nickname, Molly, according to the whims of her parents. This became important when her mother and father divorced, her mother had a breakdown and her father decided to relocate to Lahore in Pakistan to be closer to his family. All of the children followed their father abroad, occasionally visiting Louise throughout the year, after Sajad claimed that Louise was in no mental state to support them. The teenagers then moved back in with their mother for a short while, but subsequently decided to reverse their decision. This time, however, Louise wasn't letting them go without a fight.

The elder siblings ultimately returned to their father, but Louise fled to the island of Stornoway with Misbah, aka Molly, and tried to start a new life under the radar where Sajad and his family couldn't find them. There, Louise and Molly lived together for a few years, with the child registered under the name Molly Campbell, attending a local school. Louise met another man and had another daughter with him. They seemed like a new, fully settled family.

But after a while, Molly's siblings tracked her down. They came to Stornoway, met her at the gates after school one day, and persuaded her to come to Pakistan with them. In an interview with the *Guardian* many years later, Molly conceded that she did agree to go to Lahore – but that she didn't take any of the situation seriously. 'I was just a child,' she reminded the reporter, which everyone else seemed to have long forgotten as she was lined up in the middle between her parents for a good old-fashioned game of tug of war.

And that's where the media storm begins. Molly never said goodbye to her mother when she agreed to go to Pakistan; she just left, that minute, with her father and her older sister. Louise went straight to the police, claiming that Molly had been kidnapped on her way back home, and the child's face was splashed across newspapers nationwide. Where had Molly Campbell gone? Who had taken her? How had she set out in her school uniform that morning and ended up, a few hours later, on an outbound flight from Heathrow? What was a Scottish-sounding girl like Molly Campbell doing being whisked away by a man called Sajad Rana? All too soon, an 'us versus them' mentality was being whipped up.

A few days after the initial scare, Misbah Rana appeared at

that press conference in Lahore. She said that her mother had forced her to do things she didn't want to do, and that her real home was in Pakistan. Her father Sajad was standing beside her, watching over her every word. It was unclear whether she was just saying what she'd been told to say. People claimed that she had no freedom to express her wishes, and that she was being held against her will in her father's village. Nobody could work it out. Then, all of a sudden, the conference was over, and Misbah went back to Sajad's home with Omar, Adam and Tahmina. She didn't see her mother Louise for years.

The legal case concerning Misbah-or-Molly's whereabouts raged on in the background. Scottish law stated that the girl was too young to make her own decisions and should be returned to the UK, where proper court proceedings could rule on custody. In Pakistan one sharia court where Sajad had lawyers claimed that Louise was an 'apostate' under Islamic law for living with her boyfriend in sin. Another Pakistani court found in Louise's favour. None of it ended up mattering. Sajad made it clear that he was not going to bring his little girl back to Scotland, and Misbah started attending school in Pakistan.

It was not until Molly was 16 that she came back to the UK, and now she lives with her mother, although she maintains a close relationship with her father as well. She says that she will probably never return to Pakistan, despite looking back on her time there with fondness rather than fear – and although she says that she was influenced by her father, none of it was as sinister as so many journalists would have you believe.

THE VERDICT

Was Sajad within his rights to move countries, and take his children with him, after divorcing Louise, even though the kids had been primarily raised in Scotland? Should Louise's breakdown have been factored in to her losing the children in the first place?

At the heart of Molly's story is a family breakdown, a father desperate to reunite his youngest child with her brothers and sister, a mother whose love for her daughter led to her trying to begin a new life, and a media circus intent on stirring up racial tension. Needless to say, an arranged marriage was never actually on the cards – that turned out to be a bizarre and vicious rumour.

SO WHAT CAN I DO?

- If a parent suspects that their child is going to be taken out of the country by the other parent, without their consent, they should consider instructing a family lawyer immediately to get a preventative court order to stop their child being taken. You should be able to get legal aid for this. If you can't, go to any court and they will point you in the right direction or to someone who can help!

- It may be necessary to apply to have the child made a ward of court, so that the court becomes a legal guardian of the child and can exercise its powers to support its decisions on what is in your child's best interests.

- The charity Reunite gives good practical advice, supported by an information pack, to parents in this situation as to how best to prevent abduction and how to proceed if your child has been taken out of the country. (Find their address in the Appendix.)

- It may be advisable for you to contact the Identity and Passport Service (formally known as the UK Passport Service), with copies of any UK court orders. They may be able to refuse applications for the grant of a passport for your child.

- If you suspect that your child has been abducted, or is about to be taken abroad by the other parent, you should contact the police immediately. The police can, if they believe the threat is real and imminent, institute a 'Port Alert' at all UK points of departure through the National Ports Office.

- If your child has already been removed from the country the police, through Interpol, may be able to establish the port of departure and destination.

- If the parent intending to take your child out of the country is not British, they may be able to get a passport for the child from their own embassy, high commission or consulate in this country and it may be worth contacting those offices to request that they do not issue a passport. They are under no obligation to comply with the request, but may do so.

- If your child has been taken to another country, contact should be made with the Consular Directorate at the Foreign and Commonwealth Office (FCO) who can tell you whether the country that your child has been taken to has joined the Hague Convention on International Child Abduction and will give advice as to what you can do. The 1980 Hague Convention on the Civil Aspects of International Child Abduction is an agreement between various countries which aims to ensure the return of an abducted child to the country where they normally live, so that issues of residence and contact can be decided by the courts of that country.

- You should then contact the Central Authority who will handle the case. They may be able to make an application on your behalf under the Hague Convention to the foreign Central Authority. (Addresses can be found in the Appendix.)

- If your child has been taken to a country that is not a signatory to the Hague Convention, there may be no international systems in place to assist you. In such cases, you could try to come to an agreement with the other parent or start legal proceedings in the courts overseas. This is, in every sense, the worst-case scenario. The UK government cannot interfere in foreign court proceedings and cannot guarantee that your child will be returned to the UK.

CHILD MAINTENANCE

A cardinal rule of my court is this: 'If you make them, you pay for them.' If you decided to make a child (yes, you decided), then it is up to you to do everything in your power to pay for that child. Yes, that means going without things yourself! If you can afford to spend £8 per day on cigarettes then don't tell me that you do not have enough money to pay adequate child support. Your absolute primary responsibility is to ensure that your child is adequately cared for. This is not the responsibility of other taxpayers either. Before you say, 'But Judge Rinder, what on earth do you know about the real world?', let me tell you that I am a product of a broken marriage. My father was a taxi driver and my mother struggled to make her small business successful. Both could have sat on their behinds and expected others to step in. Except like the majority of decent parents in this country their entire motivation was to ensure that their children were adequately cared for. Read on to find out what to do in the event that your partner thinks that paying for your child is someone else's responsibility!

Anna's story

Isn't the gap year a wonderful thing? It is a chance to shape yourself, to travel the world, to get an insightful understanding of other cultures. I've always been a staunch advocate of that once-in-a-lifetime opportunity to get really up close and personal with everything another country has to offer. Unless, of course, you get so up close and personal that somebody ends up accidentally pregnant. Because the one real drawback of teenagers just leaving school, hormones a gogo, is that they do tend, every now and then, to confuse exchanges of culture with exchanges of bodily fluids.

This is exactly what happened in our next case, which concerns one twenty-something New Zealander – let's call her Anna – who was in the wrong place at the wrong time when another twenty-something Englishman – let's call him

James – walked into a bar. It sounds like the beginning of a joke, but instead it turned out to be the beginning of a very unusual custody case.

In this legal battle, the young couple met while Anna was waitressing in England, and got on as well as most good-looking foreign waitresses in their twenties tend to get on with most English boys in their local town. Let's just say their relationship quite literally started with a bang. Once the two young lovers had sealed the deal, they planned to travel the world together, visiting the local museum exhibits, sampling international cocktails and, of course, playing horizontal Twister at a variety of hostels every few nights. It sounded like their own perfect version of heaven in a badly ventilated dorm. But all wasn't destined to end up as carefree as they'd originally intended.

Within a month, an unexpected development reared its head: Anna was pregnant. Goodbye, margaritas in Budapest and working through the Kama Sutra together in eastern climes. Instead, a tiny half-Kiwi little girl was pushed out into the world that her parents had barely managed to explore. She was the very definition of a love child, but there wasn't going to be any love lost in the legal process that decided her fate.

The couple initially tried to make it work for their little girl: they lived on the North Island of New Zealand with the mother's parents, and then in East Anglia with the father's parents when that arrangement didn't work out in perfect harmony. Eventually, however, it was pretty clear that the whole relationship was doomed to failure. Anna packed up her things, including the baby, and told James: 'It's not East Anglia, it's you.'

James, for his part, wasn't letting his baby go without a fight. He tried to wrench the little girl from her arms, and Anna kicked him – hard. James called the police. Lawyers got involved. Everyone ended up in a courtroom, and lawyers even tried to get the parents of the youngsters to talk sense into their children, but to no avail. Eventually, a judge in London ruled on the side of the mother: The baby was to be taken back to New Zealand by Anna, although James would have visitation rights whenever he could make it to the other side of the world. Truly the ultimate cautionary tale to tell all gilet-clad gap yah boys who use the term 'banter' without irony and think that what happens on a beach in Thailand won't one day come back to haunt them.

THE VERDICT

This is a strange case in many ways, as the baby was unplanned and the parents were young. Did their age, and the fact that they were never married, change the way a judge saw their custody battle? And why did a UK judge rule in favour of removing the baby from the UK, in the arms of a New Zealander mother, when everyone knows that Australia and New Zealand combined have less culture than the probiotic yoghurt at the back of my fridge? And can James be forced to continue a relationship with his baby or pay child support to her, even if she is resident in a country thousands of miles away, or can he safely (but obviously immorally) go 'deadbeat dad' on his gap-year romance?

SO WHAT CAN I DO?

- When parents divorce, end their civil partnership or separate from their partner, agreement should be made about their child or children's future, including child maintenance payments. For those who do not know, child maintenance is financial support towards the child's everyday living costs.

- Where both parents agree (*and you should always try to*), this is termed a 'family-based arrangement'. It has the advantage that no one else is involved, it allows for flexibility if circumstances change, and it avoids the stress and expense of solicitors, court and bureaucracy.

- Where parents cannot agree, and mediation has been unsuccessfully tried, a court can rule where the children will live, when they'll spend time with each parent, and who will pay child maintenance (www.gov.uk/arranging-child-maintenance-yourself)

- Where parents cannot agree financial maintenance they can seek advice from Child Maintenance Options, an independent advice service provided on behalf of the Department for Work and Pensions. If agreement still cannot be made parents can contact the statutory Child Maintenance Service (CMS). It is obligatory for parents to first talk with Child Maintenance Options before they can apply to the CMS. Details of both can be found on the internet.

- Just to be clear: the CMS is the new rebranded name for the dreadful Child Support Agency (CSA). Anybody who has ever watched my courtroom knows exactly what I thought of this agency. They were, in many cases, about as useful as a fart in a spacesuit. In one case I dealt with, the CSA ordered Dad to pay £5 per month towards his child. Many parents spend between £20 and £50 per week on nappies alone! Yet the CSA thought that this is what this particular father could afford. Needless to say I would have ordered substantially more.

- Since 2012, the CMS can do any of the following:
  1. Try to find an absent 'paying parent' if the parent with the child does not know where they live, to sort out child maintenance.
  2. Establish how much child maintenance should be paid.
  3. Arrange for the 'paying parent' to pay child maintenance.
  4. Pass payments on to the 'receiving parent' – the parent who has main day-to-day care of the child.
  5. Look at the payments again when changes in parents' circumstances are reported.
  6. Review the payment amount every year.
  7. Take action if payments aren't made.

Application and enforcement charges are applicable, as are fees for collecting and paying out child maintenance if that service is used.

RINDER'S RULES

- REMEMBER: IF YOU MAKE THEM, YOU PAY FOR THEM!

- If you end up in court fighting over money for your children, one or both of you has failed as a parent.

- Never (and I mean never) withhold the money you are required to pay for your child as a means of bargaining for custody or in order to punish your ex-spouse. That money is for your children. I assure you, it will never work out well in the end. Just come to my court and try to explain your actions. Good luck!

CHAPTER 7

BORROWING

The majority of the cases that I hear in my courtroom, without doubt, are between people suing each other over bad loans. It is the single biggest reason for the breakdown in friendships and families. When people lend money to family and friends, it really isn't only about the cash; it is often a demonstration of their trust and love towards each other. When the borrower fails to make agreed repayments, therefore, both parties are most often left angry and bitter. The unpaid loan stops being about the money and becomes instead about the relationship itself. These arguments are often utterly toxic and result in disputes between loved ones which can go on for decades! Everybody knows my views on this topic, but for those of you who haven't seen my programme (and I trust you have a good reason for missing it), I shall repeat them. NEVER LEND MONEY TO FAMILY OR FRIENDS UNLESS YOU ARE HAPPY TO LOSE IT.

DODGY LOANS BETWEEN FAMILY AND FRIENDS

It is quite simple. Relationships rarely survive a situation where a family member or friend fails to return money they owe. As I often say, it is usually possible to make more money; it is impossible to recover the time you lose in not speaking to a loved one.

Tory Fisk

Given the risk, you might ask why anyone would lend their friend money in the first place – but then where does it stop? Anybody might chuck their friend a cup of sugar, or lend them a tenner to pay the taxi fare on their way into town. But if you're making friends with the wrong kinds of people, this can spiral out of control pretty fast. One day you're subsidising their gourmet jar of pesto in Waitrose, and the next you're bankrolling their ugly conservatory extension with the built-in solar panels. By the following year, when you're sitting on the hideous semi-outdoor furniture between those glass walls, sipping a smoothie your old friend made you with his swanky new smoothie-maker, you might end up rolling your eyes and wondering why he can afford to spend his cash on machines that make posh versions of baby food but can't afford to pay you back for that damned conservatory. He mentions how he's now thinking of buying himself a full set of 'bargain' copper-plated pans, and your blood starts to boil. Spiteful words are exchanged, and before you know it, those solar panels you hate so much are drenched in liquefied banana. Nobody in the world wants to see that sort of suburban smoothie-based warfare.

This is the sort of sad fate that befell one man called Tory

Fisk when he decided to trust his friend Jed with his hard-earned $800. Jed and Tory were good friends who went back a long way, and they both survived on fairly menial salaries. Tory – very sensibly – did not think that money and friends should mix, and was reluctant to say yes when Jed first asked. But, he said, Jed was manipulative – he told him he was his 'best friend in the whole world' and that 'if the roles were reversed, I would do the same for you'. He also told Tory that he needed money for 'essentials like food', and nobody wants to be put in the position of letting somebody starve on their watch – at least nobody who isn't on the psychopathy spectrum. Tory agreed to lend Jed the money, and Jed told him that he would pay it back in $50 monthly instalments. It seemed like a done deal.

But, it turned out, Jed wasn't overly concerned with getting the money back in his friend's bank account. He missed the first repayment that he'd promised to make – and then he missed the second. Tory was annoyed, but thought his friend might still be in a bit of a fix. Not so, it soon seemed. The next month, Tory passed Jed in the street and was startled to see that he was wearing a brand-new expensive designer suit.

'I need to look good to potential employers,' Jed told his friend, in a tone about as trustworthy as a cheating husband uses when he comes home stinking of cheap Dior-imitation perfume with somebody else's thong hanging out the end of his jeans. Tory nodded and quietly disbelieved him. 'As time went on,' he told the online magazine AlterNet, 'I found myself feeling more and more critical about his lifestyle. It was like, if I'm supporting you, then I have a stake in your choices. You're supposed to use that money to get back on your feet – not to enjoy yourself.'

Herein lies the problem with loans between friends and family members. The moment you send some cash their way, most people can't help but feel that that gives you a bit of control over the other person's life. Smoothie-makers and designer suits that you otherwise would have politely ignored suddenly become huge issues of contention. When you never used to give two monkeys about what your sister-in-law did with her spare time, you end up wondering why she's spending money on taking her two chubby kids to Thorpe Park rather than making them run around the back garden a few times, which you've privately begun to think might be a much better option for them. There's no stopping this sort of thinking: once you've started to judge another person's choices, it's a slippery slope to sending them an itemised itinerary of every bad decision they've made in the last year on the most passive-aggressive Excel document ever sent (bonus points if you add in 'marrying my brother' under 'Thorpe Park tickets' on the spreadsheet).

So Tory was thrust into the position of judging Jed's lifestyle, and it only got worse. After a while, Jed started asking Tory out for dinner and drinks – and, when Tory refused, Jed would offer to pay for him as well. Which is all very well and good, until you consider that he was offering to stump up for Tory's meal essentially with Tory's own money. A pretty transparent scam if ever there was one, and about as genuinely generous as an email from Nigeria telling you you've been left £80 million by a relative 12 times removed and the sender just needs all the details of your bank account to transfer it.

Months went by, and Jed remained unemployed. He'd needed the money from Tory in the first place because of his jobless situation, but he wasn't exactly working to remedy it – apart from, of course, sinking his best friend's cash into buying suit jackets from Armani. He was a qualified programmer and refused to apply for any jobs that weren't directly related to programming. Considering that he was $800 down and struggling with money himself, Tory thought Jed should rethink the whole thing and look outside his comfort zone. Jed, however, refused to 'lower himself' by applying for jobs that didn't fit his strict criteria, which of course is supremely ironic in every single way. He also didn't see why Tory should get a say in his major life decisions, like who he applied to work for, while Jed was increasingly beginning to see it very differently.

Eventually, it became clear to Tory that Jed was never going to find gainful employment without somebody else frog-marching him into it. And this is where I somewhat lose sympathy with our friend Tory Fisk: he decided to start a small business, with Jed and himself at the helm. Yes, he staked his future career on a man who couldn't pull together a casual $50 loan repayment to a friend each month.

Can anyone guess what happens next? That's right: Jed ruined the business. His complete lack of economic awareness meant that the whole project tanked, and Tory was left picking up the pieces of his friend's bad decisions all over again. That, combined with the conveniently forgotten loan, was the final nail in the coffin of the two men's friendship. And really, Tory should be grateful that it ended so soon, before he could find himself penniless on the side of a road in Las Vegas, wondering what happened to the house he once owned and watching the fumes of Jed's sparkling new Ferrari slowly dissipate into the desert air.

SO WHAT CAN I DO?

So what can you do if your friend is a bit of a Jed and you've made the mistake of entrusting them with your hard-earned cash? Is there anything you can do before you hand it over that gives you more of a guarantee that they'll make their repayments?

How do you cope with turning a friendship into a professional affair? And should you have confidence that the law will back you up if your mate does a runner, or should you instead stick with the old adage not to lend anything out that you expect to get back?

I am afraid I am going to repeat myself more than once and I really do not care. It is a warning which has come down through history so it is worth listening to: as William Shakespeare put it, 'Never a borrower or a lender be!'

I do understand that life is not always as simple as that, and that sometimes we are put in a position where we feel obliged to lend money when asked to by a friend or family member. It is quite likely that lending money is the last thing you want to do but your innate decency is bombarded with feelings of obligation, sympathy, loyalty, love and – most commonly – guilt. You may even feel that if you do not stump up, the alternative may be loan sharks or payday loan companies, with their enormous interest rates plunging the borrowers even deeper in the mire.

As long as you are very aware of the risks of never seeing your money again, or potentially destroying a relationship, go ahead. People will keep lending money and people will keep thinking that losing that money or that friend will never happen to them.

Lending money to a friend or family member

If you insist on lending money to family or friends in need, then the absolute non-negotiable moron-avoidance rule is this: GET EVERTHING IN WRITING. You will have to prove to a court that a legally enforceable loan exists between you and the other person. In order to do this, you will be asked to produce some kind of documentary evidence or (in nearly all cases) the court will come to the view that there was no legally binding agreement between the two of you, in other words that it was an informal arrangement which was never intended to go to court in the event that things went wrong.

- Really think about it. Do not do this on a whim. Certainly not when you've had a couple of glasses of wine. You will regret it.

- Can you afford it? Don't lend money if you aren't in a strong financial position yourself. If you were suddenly to lose your job in a month's time, would you be able to survive without the money you are about to lend? If not, do not even consider a loan.

- Can they afford it? No one really likes talking about money, even with close family or friends, but you are going to have to be as sure as you can be that they will be able to pay when they say they will. Ask them outright about their financial situation. Do they earn a stable wage? What other financial commitments do they have? How good are they generally about managing their money? If they cannot get a bank loan because of bad credit, do you really want to be lending them money? What is the money actually going to be used for? It's down to you how probing you are. You are going to have to use your own judgement about whether this is all a good idea or not.

- It's a good idea to check with your spouse before you make this decision, particularly if you are sharing a bank account. All kinds of extremely serious arguments can arise if you don't.

- Being a good friend or a loving family member means putting the other person's best interests first, and sometimes that might result in you refusing to lend them the money. It might, for example, enable them to carry on bad habits. Declining a loan to an alcoholic, a substance abuser or a gambler may be easy to rationalise. However, people have other problems that money alone will not fix. A better thing to do might be to give them your time instead, teaching them money management skills or helping them sort out their finances. You could point them in the direction of the Citizens Advice Bureau or your local-authority money-advice service to help them consolidate their debts. Sometimes you have got to be cruel to be kind.

- If you are going to do this properly and safely, by following all my tips, you need to be sure you can put in the time needed to set up the agreement, to monitor payments etc. The more safeguards you adopt (and therefore the more time you put in), the less likely it is that something will go irrevocably wrong.

- Like Tory and Jed above, seriously have a think about how you will feel if you don't think they are spending your money wisely. If they said it was for fixing a boiler, and the next thing you know they are off to Paris for a naughty weekend, how will you react to this? Can you stay neutral or will you turn into a less eloquent (and far less brilliant) version of Judge Rinder? Even if they do pay you back, will you resent them for this in the future?

Set the terms of the loan

- Provide your friend or loved one with a timeline of when the money should be paid back, whether in a lump sum or in instalments. If you agree to instalments, tell them exactly when you want each instalment and how much is to be paid each time. If you do not tell them when you need the money back, it's easy for the borrower to not pay up. There aren't the fees for late payment, higher interest rates and negative impact on credit scores that come with a standard bank loan, so the borrower probably won't feel any urgency to pay. If you let them know exactly when you need the money back and give them a schedule for how it is to be paid, it adds more formality.

- Discuss the possible problems that could arise between you and the borrower at the outset. Say something like 'I've heard so many horror stories about loaning money. I will be hurt and it could really change our relationship if this doesn't work out. How can we try to stop that happening?' Be open and frank about this. It might seem awkward but could save so much heartbreak and hassle down the line.

- If you lend money for a reasonable length of time, like a year or six months, and you don't charge interest, you are effectively losing money, even in these times of tiny interest rates. The money was probably in savings account and earning a bit of interest, so by taking it out and giving it to someone else, interest-free, you won't be earning that interest. It may be complicated to think about, but if it is a large sum of money, charging interest is something you should maybe consider. The amount of interest will most likely be lower than that of formal loan providers, but it could cover most of what you would lose, and may increase the motivation of the borrower to pay you back on time. If you do receive any interest on a loan, then you have to inform HM Revenue & Customs, as this amount may be liable for taxation as income.

Get it in writing! Sorry, I need to write that in big: GET IT ON PAPER

- Draw up a written agreement or contract with all the terms you have discussed above – the amount, when it's to be paid, instalments, interest, collateral, what happens if the loan is not paid, and anything else you've agreed on. This is so both of you are clear on what you have agreed, and also to save you when it all goes horribly wrong.

- Make sure you specify who the parties are, with full names and addresses. Make the agreement as clear and concise as possible. It does not have to be full of legal language. Just make sure it says exactly what you have both agreed. Have the word 'loan' written in the agreement, so that it can never be alleged that the money was merely a gift. Picture yourself months down the line when the loan hasn't been paid and you are relying on this written agreement in court. If you are sure that the court could not have any doubt as to what the terms of the loan consisted of, then the written agreement is clear enough. If there is any margin of doubt, rewrite it.

- There are sample loan agreements online, some free, some you have to pay for. They may also be called a 'promissory note'. Be sure to check what kind of website they are on and whether it is a UK website or not. Lots of them are from the US where the law is different.

- Make sure both of you sign and date the agreement, in the presence of an independent witness.

- If the loan is a large amount of money, it might make sense to have a solicitor look over the agreement to make sure you've got everything down that should be there.

- A loan agreement is especially important if the borrower is possibly a little bit long in the tooth. It might be unpleasant to think about, but if the borrower were to die, you would need a written agreement to be able to get your money back from their estate. In fact, anyone can drop down dead at any moment (a cheerful thought for you there) so do it even if the borrower isn't your granny.

Show me the money!

- When it comes to actually transferring the money, do it in a way that can be recorded, e.g. by cheque or bank transfer. Avoid cash like the plague.

- If you are paying a bill or debt directly, get a receipt or confirmation that you have paid. This is both so that you are both covered if the borrower says you never paid, and also if whoever you are paying the bill to raises an issue because it wasn't the debt-holder who paid.

- It would be a good idea to get the borrower to set up a standing order for repayments, and then ask them to show you confirmation from their bank that they have done this.

- Check with your bank that these repayments are actually happening. Contacting the borrower early on is far better than down the line, when they are even further in debt.

- If you decide not to have a standing order, keep a meticulous record of when any money is paid and by what method (cash, cheque etc.). It might be a good idea for both of you to sign the record when the money is handed over.

- If any changes to the repayment plan are made, however small, like changing the amount of money in each instalment, go back and amend your agreement. Again, both of you should sign it in front of an independent witness.

- Finally, if you have bags of cash and friends and family are coming out of the woodwork asking for loans, be aware that if you lend money regularly (and are making money out of it) you may need to be licensed by the Financial Conduct Authority (FCA). If you aren't making money, and you feel like you are being taken advantage of, remember you can always say no. Lending money to one family member does not mean you have to lend it to every second cousin four times removed. It's your money.

Too late, the deed is done my friend owes me money and I want it back.

Nobody wants to be *that person* who constantly has to nag about being paid back. These are your family and friends; you might not want to put either yourself or them in an awkward situation. You have taken the choice to lend the money, therefore you have to deal with the fact that if they don't pay up when you want them to, you are going to have to ask for it back. No one else is going to do it for you. Don't go in all guns blazing, though. Gentle reminders may work better than aggressive threats.

The borrower may feel embarrassed about not being able to pay. It might not simply be a case of them not wanting to pay up. They may be in real hardship, and feel they can't talk to you. You should approach them in such a way as to not make them feel bad. They may already feel awful about having had to ask you for money in the first place, and are now ashamed they can't pay. They are your friend for a reason, and you obviously liked and trusted them enough to give them a loan in the first place. Be approachable and willing to listen.

Sarah, Liam and the disappearing £3,000 – a cautionary tale

Sarah and Liam had been together for three and a half years when he asked her the question every girl wants to hear: 'Baby, can you lend me £3,000 to cover my credit-card debts?' OK, so it wasn't the most romantic of situations, but Sarah trusted him. After all, you don't spend three and a half years whispering sweet nothings in somebody's ear in order to scam them out of a few thousand pounds. You would (I would have thought) at least want a sugar daddy and a sizeable slice of a million-pound house for that sort of investment of time.

But as it turned out – and it always does turn out this way – Liam was about as trustworthy as a box of economy burgers. A couple of months after he'd cleared up his debt problems, he decided that Sarah wasn't as exciting as she was when she had money that he wanted to borrow, and promptly walked out. Despite having promised her that he would repay the money 'very soon' after taking it, he hadn't stumped up any cash while he was with her. Magically, he seemed to have forgotten about that whole thing while they were still sharing a bed – and, being in a relationship with the man at the time, Sarah had sensitively decided not to mention it.

The break-up, however, seemed like a good time to sort out the outstanding money issue before parting ways – or so Sarah thought. She approached Liam about her covering him for his little credit card problem, and he immediately denied that any loan arrangement between them had taken place. She must be mistaken, he claimed, as he'd never take £3,000 from his girlfriend. She must just be mixing up the whole story with some crazy dream she had.

Predictably, Sarah wasn't amused by this complete moron's lack of explanation. She knew that she might have some legal power, but was worried about the fact that the two had been boyfriend and girlfriend when she gave Liam the money. She'd heard that people could argue in court after a bad break-up that a loan was really a gift during the relationship, and therefore never needed paying back. And, of course, because she'd been in a long-term partnership with Liam at the time, she'd never thought to formalise the agreement in the first place: no letters were signed, no contracts were drawn up, so there was no written proof that the loan was ever agreed. It was his word against hers.

THE VERDICT

The reason that this is a cautionary tale is that – sadly – Sarah lost her money. A court found no evidence that the cash had been a loan. Had Sarah read this book or ever watched my court I doubt she would have lost her case. It's such a shame that I wasn't sitting as a TV judge when she took her case to court. I feel (even without her producing evidence) that I would have made mincemeat out of Liam. Lucky Liam. . . He is one that has sadly slipped through my net.

SO WHAT CAN I DO?

- Courts understand that loans between loved ones often are informal, and normal, everyday people (i.e. non-lawyers) do not always jump to the conclusion that everything needs to be in writing, particularly when they love and trust the person they are giving a loan to. So if you didn't write anything down, don't think all is lost. You may still be able to get the money back by going to court. It is just going to be more difficult for you.

- If you end up in court, the judge will decide whether, on balance, the money was a proper legally enforceable loan or whether it was merely a gift. There is the presumption in law that when money is lent between family members there was never any intention to take the matter to court in the event that things went wrong. This in law is called 'an intention to create legal relations'. If there was no intention to create legal relations then you do not have a contract and the loan is unenforceable. The court would find that the money you gave was nothing more than a generous gift.

- Before you go to court, try to find any evidence to show that a loan was made rather than gift: bank statements, emails, texts, anything at all. The fact that you were not in the habit of giving large amounts of money as gifts might be useful. Or if you had given a loan to the borrower before, can you show through bank statements that you gave money which was repaid?

- Give the borrower a chance to pay the money back, maybe in smaller instalments or for a longer period. Being amenable now may save you having to go down the legal route later on.

- If all else fails, and the borrower has legged it, or you just can't get the money back, you are going to need to take them to court. If you have your papers in order (and you are lucky enough) you could even bring them before my court!

- If the value of the debt is less than £10,000, you should go to the small claims court. Please see the chapter on how to make a claim at the small claims court for help.

If the loan is above this amount, you should ask a solicitor to help you, or, again, go to the CAB for advice. Many times, the threat alone of going to court is enough to make someone pay up.

RINDER'S RULES

- Do not lend friends or family money unless you are prepared to lose it.

- If you must give a friend of family member a loan, make sure you get it in writing, setting out everything clearly. READ THIS CHAPTER CAREFULLY.

- When things go wrong, do not act like a bull in a china shop. First find out why the friend or relative cannot pay and attempt to come to an alternative arrangement.

- If you end up in court, make sure you prepare your evidence carefully. Get everything you have on paper. Just like me, most judges prefer paper over people. As the saying goes: that which cannot speak cannot lie!

Please be aware that this chapter does not deal with loans from professional or commercial lenders such as banks or (even worse) payday lenders. If you end up in serious debt with them, you need to deal with the situation as soon as possible. Do not bury your head in the sand. The good news is that you have powerful legal rights over these lenders and, in many cases, this debt can be renegotiated or written off. If you find yourself in this situation get in touch with either the government's website or the CAB, whose addresses can be found at the end of this book.

CHAPTER 8

LEAVING PROPERTY WHEN YOU DIE

L ast year I was asked to advise *Sun* readers on my top legal tips for Christmas. The editor was expecting something festive: make sure you buy your presents from a reputable supplier, that sort of thing. He was a little surprised by my response. Rather than suggesting that people ought to keep their receipts (although that is an absolute must, of course), I advised readers to make sure that they had sorted their wills out at once. I was not suggesting this because the murder rate between spouses rockets at this time of year (although that is actually true) but because if you don't get your affairs in order before you croak, there is a chance that a family member you cannot stand will get your hard-earned property.

Of all the cases that lawyers deal with, disputes between families over inheritance are some of the most bitter and ugly. Years ago these fights were rather rare, but as we have become a nation of homeowners there is a good chance that your family house is a worth a small fortune, which increases the chances of feuding when you die. The best way to avoid these sordid squabbles is to set out clearly what you intend to happen to your property by making a will. This is not necessarily the end of the matter but is usually the best way of stopping people crawling out of the woodwork when they discover you have left a valuable asset. This is not always entirely straightforward, however. Your wife will be able to apply to have your will set aside, for example, if you leave your dog everything and expect her to move in to the family kennel (regardless of whether she was a total harridan or not).

If you end up in some sort of conflict over an estate (which is worth more than £10,000) then I would strongly advise you to seek professional advice at once. As you will discover, the law relating to estates (called 'probate') is extremely complicated. You'd be a complete fool to try and pursue the case yourself!

I understand that this is a pretty macabre thing to think about; after all, why should you care what happens after you're six feet under? The best reply I always give in response to that attitude is this: in the event that your family ends up fighting, almost everything will end up in the pockets of lawyers. Still thinking of not making a will?! In this chapter you will read some horror stories of what happens when families have failed to follow my advice.

The family who spent their inheritance fighting each other

We begin with a story of siblings who couldn't agree on their mother's final intentions, mainly because, surprisingly enough, each one believed Mother had intended to favour them. It started, as it always does, with three perfect children: Libby, Julia and Peter. The kiddies of two proud parents, each separated by two years, these siblings always seemed to get along famously.

Libby was the oldest, a kindly girl with ambitions to start a family early, who ended up as a single mother on a council estate with four young children. Julia, the second oldest, was always known as the clever one, and went straight to law school before qualifying as a magistrate. Peter, the baby of the family, was helped through the latter part of his education and his early job problems by Julia, and ended up settling into an entrepreneurial role at the head of his own highly successful recruitment business.

The children finally settled and lived markedly different lives, but they never forgot where they had come from. In an article for the *Telegraph* in 2013, Peter recalled how his parents had emphasised the importance of fairness in their lives: every Christmas present was counted throughout their childhoods to make sure all three children got an exactly equal amount, and when Libby alone was offered a bicycle by an aunt, her parents turned it down because it would have seemed unfair. Everything they had was split three ways. In adulthood, however, this principle went flying out the window with enviable speed. What used to be a harmonious family unit operating well away from the limelight ended up in a catastrophic court case that dominated the national headlines, turned brother against sister, and spent all of the money the family had stood to gain.

But let's rewind for a second, and trace it back to where everything – and everybody – started. When the children grew up and moved out of the safety and security of their parents' modest home, their different paths became very obvious. Libby was still living penniless on an estate in London. Julia was comfortably set up in the suburbs with a five-bedroom house with a swimming pool, a husband and two daughters. Peter was married to a Canadian wife who owned an internet business (an excellent financial complement to his own recruitment business, no doubt) that she sold for £4.9 million at the peak of its success, leading to a huge payout for shareholders. Peter's wife had employed two of Libby's children in the company, and they walked away with some of the money themselves. That, according to Peter, was when the green-eyed monster began to get to Julia.

By this time, Libby, Julia and Peter were in their middle age. Their father had died and their mother was in ailing health. She had made a will in 1996 based on the tradition of fairness and equality that had defined her offspring's childhoods: each would get a third of the inheritance, whatever became of them and whatever money they made in their own endeavours. In 2000 her health began to decline more rapidly, and in 2006 Peter (as the most financially solvent) agreed to buy her a bungalow near to Julia so that Mum could live close enough to be cared for by her daughter when the time came.

Once Mum lived near to Julia, things began to change. Tensions arose around her health and the issues that it threw up, and Peter and Julia began to argue. At one point, Julia's husband gave Mum a highly sugary drink in front of everyone, even though she was severely diabetic. Peter, shocked, ripped the drink away and called Julia's husband an idiot in front of his daughter. This was the beginning of the end. Julia responded in the severest way a British person possibly can respond to a highly personal insult: she sent a strongly worded email.

By the time a few emails had been exchanged, the relationship between Julia and Peter had been irrevocably damaged. They stopped speaking for a number of years: the brother and sister who had once sat at desks poring over Peter's O-level books seemed to have severed their connection for ever. However, in 2007 there was a turning point: their mother had a stroke, and both seemed to realise that life was too short to hold on to petty grievances. Peter and Julia were reconciled, while Libby remained on the sidelines, resolutely failing to offend anyone and collecting her benefits in her shabby flat without a complaint. In 2009 the siblings' mother finally died. Everyone was devastated.

It seemed like they would all pull together in this time of need, but of course everyone had overestimated Julia's moral fibre. When Libby and Peter made their respective trips down to their mother's bungalow, they found that it had already been stripped of anything of value – either financial or sentimental. Everything from photographs and mementos to jewellery and furniture had disappeared. Julia had cleared the lot.

And that wasn't all. As the siblings stood there amongst the paltry leftovers of their mother's belongings, Julia informed them that the will made in 1996 had been changed just before their mother died. In 2007, just two weeks after she had a stroke, Mum had been driven to a solicitor's office by her magistrate daughter and had signed a new will that cut Peter out entirely. Peter was shocked: although he didn't need the money, he'd always believed in that principle of ultimate fairness meted out by their parents. He refused to believe that his mother would have cut him out of her will, and, when presented with the evidence, said that he believed his mother couldn't have been in her right mind. She was ill, after all, with a medically confirmed brain injury, and she had made a detailed will splitting the inheritance three equal ways back in 1996.

Peter found himself faced with will-based legal disputes. Should he, as a multimillionaire, accept his lot and go back to his rich Canadian wife and his lavish lifestyle? Should he go with the flow and let Julia walk away with half of the inheritance, and Libby – who, unlike Peter, hadn't been cut out completely – with the other half? It seemed that Julia believed she was owed more because she'd taken care of her mother in her old age and lived beside her in the bungalow – but was that really fair? With all the objects of sentimental value fresh in his mind, Peter decided that it absolutely was not. There was only one thing for it. He was going to take his older sister to court.

Peter told Libby about his plan, and, to his initial surprise, she said that she was with him. She agreed that what Julia had done was unfair, and seemed underhand, even though she personally stood to inherit less if Peter won. And if you're thinking that Libby seems like the eternal Cinderella in this story, yes, I'm thinking the same thing too. Maybe if she'd inherited even a smidgen of Julia's deviousness, she'd have ended up with the five-bedroom house instead of the council flat – but I suppose we'll never know.

Peter said he felt sick about taking Julia to court, but he didn't know what else to do. He wanted to prove to himself that Mum loved him just as much as his other siblings, and everyone knows that the best place to do that is in a court of law! So he and Libby went to court to investigate just what had been going on between Julia and her mother in the intervening years – and, in doing so, they opened a whole other can of worms. Because it turned out that Julia hadn't just been in the business of creatively managing wills with her persuasive magistrate influence. She had also been doing a bit of an Artful Dodger on her mother's bank account.

'What exactly had gone on?' I hear you cry. Well, £18,000 had gone on – and that included £289 on a nice day out at a Formula One race for Julia and her husband, as well as £854 paying off their daughter's credit card. Over the years, Julia had dipped in and out of her mother's account freely, presumably believing that she was entitled to all of this because she was doing the bare minimum expected morally of a human and making sure that her extremely sick mother didn't die. Perhaps she mistook herself for paid home help and her mother for an elderly client, and began taking payment for her dues. Or perhaps she'd just lost her moral compass at the same time as she lost her sense of style and social grace by buying a house with a swimming pool in Milton Keynes. Either way, it was clear that love really hadn't been enough for this daughter: she'd wanted to see her efforts reflected in cold, hard cash, and she'd made sure that she was going to do it while her mother was alive as well as well after her death.

The court case hinged on a number of different factors, and obviously Julia's case was damaged by the big reveal that she was, on the face of it, a heartless thief who had had one hand on her mother's brain medication and another on her wallet the entire time. Libby and Peter argued that their mother had not had the mental capacity to sign a will when she had made her new copy with Julia by her side in 2007, and it was up to the judge to decide whether this was a reasonable argument. The case dragged on, and ended up taking six full days in court, with 26 witnesses called to the stand. Not only that, but the legal costs piled up higher and higher with every passing hour, until eventually they'd climbed to £150,000 – *more than the entire value of the estate being contested.*

THE VERDICT

Eventually, after a long and exhausting battle, Libby and Peter won the case. The inheritance was to be split three ways equally, and Julia was ordered to repay the £18,000 she'd taken from her mother's bank account. Peter agreed to take the hit on the legal costs and donate his share of the money to Libby. Meanwhile, their mother presumably turned in her grave at everything that had happened between three children who had once seemed so close and loving.

SO WHAT CAN I DO?

So what exactly do you do when faced with a complicated case like this? Can a will really be revoked if the court decides, posthumously, that that person wasn't in their right mind when they signed it? Does it look suspect if a person changes their existing will a few years before they die, even if they do it in good faith? And is someone entitled to more from a house, a bank account or a will if they've done the lion's share of the caring when their relative fell into ill health during old age?

- Even though things went wrong in this case, do not be deterred from making a will! In most cases, the terms of a person's will are final and binding but in some cases they can be challenged.

- If you can prove that there is something wrong with the will or that there were dubious circumstances surrounding the way it was written, then it is not necessarily set in stone, which is why I always advise you to get legal advice before compiling one.

- From the outset, I want to make clear that contesting a will is likely to take a considerable amount of time, worry and expense. Cases can continue for years before being resolved.

- Consider carefully whether both the amount of money involved and the potential for irreparable damage between you and your family is actually worth it. Sometimes it might be better to suck it up and accept the decision your relative made, no matter how painful that might be.

- In any event, you cannot just contest a will because you are unhappy with what you have been given (or not given). There need to be valid grounds for contesting a will before a court will declare it is invalid and these grounds are very strictly defined.

- If a will is pronounced invalid, a prior valid will made by the testator will be the one that is used to determine where the property goes instead.

- Where no previous will exists, the intestacy rules will apply to the estate, which means that the property will first go to any surviving spouse and thereafter to surviving children; if there aren't any of them then on to brothers or sisters and so on and so forth. Consider whether you would stand to gain either from an existing previous will or under intestacy. If you aren't a next of kin, for example, you won't get anything.

- If you have any doubts about the will, you need to seek legal advice from a solicitor as soon as you can. They will investigate the circumstances around the preparation of the will, and can enter something called a caveat at the Probate Registry to prevent the distribution of the property from starting. This will give the solicitor time to properly prepare the grounds for contesting the will. It is important to act quickly to prevent the estate being administered and the assets being dished out.

- The solicitor will advise you on whether you have any grounds for contesting the will. Listen to this advice. If they tell you that your chances are low, you need to be aware of the fact that you will risk being liable to pay a percentage of the other side's legal fees as well as your own if you choose to proceed. In a probate case, especially one lasting for years, you could be looking at hundreds of thousands of pounds.

What grounds might you have for contesting a will?

The first ground available to you is that the will has been improperly prepared. A will must be made in writing and be signed by the testator (the person making the will) in the presence of two witnesses who must also each attest and sign the will in the presence of the testator. Alternatively the will can be signed in the presence of the testator and at their direction (let's say they are on their deathbed and too ill to sign). If any of these requirements are missing, the will is invalid. The legal presumption is that a will has been made properly, and you have to prove that it was not. Unless you have evidence, this may be very difficult!

The second ground is that the testator lacked the necessary mental capacity to make a will. In other words, at the time it was written they didn't know the relative whereabouts of their bottom and their elbow. A testator *must* have fully understood that they were making a will and that the will stated how they wished to dispose of their assets when they died. They need to be fully aware of the contents of their estate, and any claims on that estate (such as loans or mortgages). The court will look at the extent of the will-maker's vulnerability or illness. Mild dementia might not automatically render a will void. A 101-year-old lady, while frail and housebound, may be deemed to have been perfectly willing and able to change her will on her 100th birthday. A person who is normally perfectly sane might have been rendered incapable by medication at the time of writing their will. The court will look into all the circumstances and make a decision. Often this will not be an easy one to make. Any evidence at all that points to the testator's mental capacity at the time the will was made will help prove your case. Again, unless the testator was certifiably gaga (and a doctor says so) you aren't going to get anywhere!

The third ground is that a testator must have knowledge of and approve of the contents of their will and they must know that they are signing a will. This ground can be used to contest a will even if it appears to be validly executed and the testator was perfectly well. So it may be that the testator was put under some kind of undue influence (a gun held to their head, for example) which would mean that the will would become void. These cases are very hard to prove and usually end up in incredibly bitter, lengthy and expensive court cases.

SO WHAT CAN I DO?

In order to make a successful allegation of undue influence, you would have to demonstrate that the testator was coerced into making the will. You would have to prove that there was some kind of manipulation, deception or intimidation by another party to put pressure on the person making the will in order to influence its content to their advantage. So you might want to conduct further investigation if your nan's dementia carer ends up with her entire estate.

The test courts use to determine if there was some kind of undue influence is whether the testator is likely to have thought: This is not my wish but I *must* do it. Although no actual physical force is necessary, you cannot get the will set aside because your scheming sister who was entirely indifferent to your grandmother during her life became more helpful when she heard that Nan was going to be preparing her will, even if it was plainly obvious what your sister's intentions were. This is incredibly hard to prove – you cannot get the testator on the stand to give evidence in court!

If you think that it's not the testator's real signature on the will, you can try to plead that the signature was forged. Again, this is really difficult to prove. An expert's assessment of the signature will be required and the two witnesses will be sought to give evidence.

When blood isn't thicker than water

Alfred and Maureen Rawlings were a sweet old couple who had two biological sons of their own, as well as another unofficially adopted one. Terry Marley had moved in to the family home as a teenager when he had nowhere else to go, and Alfred and Maureen had taken him under their wing. He had been one of their son's best friends at school, so they knew that they couldn't abandon him in his time of need. And, with a little bit of love and encouragement, Terry grew up into a fine young man.

As time went on, everything seemed peachy with the new

blended family. The kids grew up, got jobs and moved away, and when Alfred and Maureen became old and infirm, Terry remembered their kindness in his younger years and looked after them. In total, he ended up living with his adopted family for more than 30 years of his life, tending to their ailments and keeping them company in their later days.

Impressed by his devotion, which was over and above what either of their other two scrounging little biological sons had offered, Alfred and Maureen made a decision: they would leave their entire legacy of £70,000, as well as their £400,000 home in Kent, to Terry. In 1999 they went to their solicitor, drew up identical wills in each name, and signed them. Everything seemed sorted. Eleven years later, Maureen Rawlings sadly died, and Alfred passed away three years after that, having remained clear about his intentions for where the money would go once he was no longer here.

As you can imagine, the two Rawlings sons weren't exactly thrilled with that outcome. After travelling down to meet with lawyers after their father's death, they found out that both of their parents had agreed on leaving Terry Marley their full estate. The cuckoo in the nest had eaten all the eggs. It seemed to them that Terry had been playing the long game with their parents' money – and they weren't going to give up that sizeable inheritance without a fight.

Terry knew that the Rawlings kids weren't going to play ball nicely. He offered to split the £70,000 with them, but to no avail. His adoptive brothers, once his best mates on the playground, were not hankering to buddy up with him in the courtroom.

And then the Rawlings brothers made a startling discovery. The solicitor who had drawn up Alfred and Maureen's wills had messed the whole thing up: they'd accidentally signed each other's, rather than their own. This was a golden opportunity.

They took the botched wills to a judge, arguing that the wills were null and void because they hadn't been ratified in the correct way. In other words, they should be completely ignored, meaning that legally Alfred and Maureen died intestate (with no legal wills to go by).

Conveniently, that meant that the inheritance would fall automatically to the next of kin, who were, of course, the Rawlings brothers themselves. And so a legal bloodbath began, making its way through pretty much every courtroom possible until it hit the Supreme Court. Lawyers for Terry Marley had argued throughout that it was very clear what Alfred and Maureen had intended, and judges had agreed – but that didn't necessarily make it stand legally. The Rawlings brothers continued to argue that their parents should be considered to have never produced wills. Most found in their favour, and Terry Marley was repeatedly told that he couldn't or shouldn't appeal, before applying again and being allowed to go to the next legal stage. It was a tough upward struggle, but Terry believed that he was fighting for what Alfred and Maureen wanted – and, at the very end, judges in the Supreme Court unanimously agreed that their wills should be taken at face value even though they'd been signed by each other. In 2014 Terry won his battle and fully disinherited the Rawlings brothers, which I'm sure did wonders for their rapidly disintegrating relationship. The cuckoo finally crowed!

SO WHAT CAN I DO?

So, are there situations where your will might not be taken into consideration because of a clerical error, even though you knew exactly which irritating little moron was going to be cut out of your inheritance and which little beam of sunshine was going to be favoured from the grave? Can someone really fight a legal battle based upon the idea that they knew someone else's intentions, even if the legal documents aren't up to scratch? And how common are cases when the will left behind ends up favouring people who would never have qualified as legally recognised next of kin, cutting out entirely the people who thought they stood to make a fortune out of someone's death?

- A will may be rectified (i.e. altered) where it fails to carry out the testator's intentions either because of a clerical error or because of a failure on the part of the person preparing the will to understand the testator's instructions. When a will is negligently drafted this is often the first port of call before making a claim for professional negligence against the person who made the will.

- A claim may be brought if the words in a will are unclear or ambiguous. In this case the court is asked to determine the meaning of the words used in the will.

- A mistake may have been made in a will, meaning that it does not properly express the testator's wishes. If this error results in you suffering a loss as a potential beneficiary, you can apply to the court for the will to be amended (known as rectification) within six months of the date of the grant of probate.

- The Administration of Justice Act 1982 allows a will to be rectified if a court is satisfied that it does not express or carry out the testator's true intentions. There are, however, only two possible grounds for the court to use these powers:

1. Clear evidence that the will does not reflect the testator's intentions because of a typographical or clerical error (e.g. inadvertently mistyping a legacy clearly intended to be £1,000 as £100).
2. An obvious failure to understand the testator's clear instructions by whoever drew up the will.

- Your spouse cannot leave everything to Battersea Dogs Home leaving you with no option but a shady B&B and a lifetime of selling the *Big Issue*. If your husband (it usually is) has shuffled off this mortal coil without making sufficient financial provision for you, the law permits you to apply to the court to have this resolved.

- New Court of Appeal rulling (28 July 2015) would appear to open gates for 100% charity legacies to be challenged by children cut out of will.

RINDER'S RULES

- **Make a will!**
  There are lots of DIY will kits around to buy, or even free templates to use. These might be completely sufficient if your will is straightforward – if you are leaving everything to your only child, for example. If it is more complicated than that, you can still write the will yourself, but I would absolutely advise you to get a solicitor to cast their eye over it to check it is valid. This may be a short half-hour meeting and may cost (depending on where you are in the UK) less than £50.

- **Talk to your family about it**
  Having a discussion about what is going to happen to your property after you die might help later on down the line.

- **Be very clear about what you want to happen to your property**
  When you make a will, be very clear about who is getting what and what happens if relationships break down and divorces are involved. It is your will! You can make whatever kind of complicated directions you choose. If you only want to give money to your daughter-in-law on the condition that she is still married to your son, that's completely your choice to do so. Just make sure it is clearly understandable. Having a solicitor take a quick look at a draft of your will should not cost much money, and might stop your daughter-in-law getting her grubby divorced hands on your hard-earned assets.

CHAPTER 9

GETTING FIRED

When, how and if you can be given the boot is a huge area of law. This chapter does not attempt to deal with all of it. If you want precise detail I suggest you buy a text-book and do not attempt to drive or operate heavy machinery after you have read it. In this chapter I describe some extra-ordinary cases of people being wrongly fired, and set out, in general terms, what you can and should do if this happens to you.

If you take nothing else from reading this chapter then I hope you remember this: if you think you have been sacked unlawfully you need to act quickly. You cannot hang about. The employment tribunal who deals with these cases applies time limits stringently. You only have three months from the date your job was terminated to bring a claim and can only have your claim dealt with by the tribunal if you qualify in law. This means that large numbers of people in our communities (particularly those on so-called zero-hour contracts) have fewer rights as employees than the rest of us. Welcome to Britain in 2015!

Sarah's story

Nineteen-year-old Sarah Finch was a rebel without a cause. The Carmarthen-based teenager, who was studying for A levels in chemistry, physics and biology at the time, had taken a job with the local branch of McDonald's to make some extra cash. By the time she disclosed her true colours and brought everyone in West Wales to shame, she'd been working at the branch for 13 months, flipping burgers, salting fries and providing Happy Meal toys to the innocent children of the United Kingdom, all the while keeping it from the public that she was hiding a hideous secret. Because Sarah Finch, you see, was an over-sprinkler.

If you're not aware what an over-sprinkler is, well, neither was Sarah before her sound-minded bosses at McDonald's decided to point it out to her. You see, despite the fact that Sarah was a model employee – she never even complained once about the indignity of having to wear an unflattering peaked cap with a large yellow 'M' on it, or the fact that people who work in Subway get to call themselves 'Sandwich Artists' while people who work in McDonald's are, shall we say, less respected – she suffered from mindless generosity. One day, when one of her fellow employees went on a break, they took advantage of this and asked Sarah to make them a 99p McFlurry ice cream.

'How many chocolate sprinkles?' Sarah asked her friend, with a jaunty little grin. 'Ooh, Sarah, make it a nice one,' her friend replied. So Sarah, being the girl that she was, generously poured a few more sprinkles than she usually would over her colleague's delicious ice cream treat. I know what you're thinking: that crazy, stupid thief! Needless to say, word got out about Sarah's over-sprinkling qualities. You can imagine how it started: nudges in the hallway, winks behind the deep-fat fryer.

'That Sarah Finch in the Carmarthen branch – she's generous with her sprinkles, if you know what I mean,' regular McDonald's customers might have said to each other while passing on the street. 'Go to Sarah on your lunch breaks, lads,' another employee might say while coming in to work that morning at Maccy D's. 'She'll give you what you're looking for.'

It didn't take long for word to reach Sarah's employers, and once they'd heard the news, they did what any sensible person would do: they fired her on the spot. After all, a properly run McDonald's franchise is like a well-oiled military machine. One person takes a liberty, and the next thing you know, anarchy reigns. Tolerate an overstuffed McFlurry one day, or a veggie burger served without the mandatory sneer, and the next thing you know, your employees will be sailing around the back room in a river of Diet Coke on a canoe made entirely from French fries and discarded mozzarella sticks. The horror, the horror.

Sarah, however, was lacking in remorse. When she was served her notice of dismissal, with the reason stated as gross misconduct for 'giving away food without payment', she decided not to take it lying down. She knew that an over-sprinkler may be a bit of a social tearaway but is still a human being. She knew that people deserve second chances when they take their issues one McFlurry too far. And so she decided to take Carmarthen McDonald's to court.

A few months later, Sarah had found herself a lawyer and turned up at an employment tribunal accusing her ex-employers of unfair dismissal. A handful of chocolate sprinkles does not constitute as a sackable offence, she argued. That particular branch of McDonald's was run by a franchise company called Lonetree, so it was them that she and her lawyer summoned to court for a reasonable explanation and some compensation for lost earnings to boot.

Presumably because they knew how ridiculous the headlines would look, McDonald's backed down pretty quickly. In exchange for Sarah pretending that her previous employers weren't insane sprinkle police who had set up their own burger-based fascist state, they agreed to settle out of court for £3,000. As part of the terms of the settlement, Sarah would also be guaranteed a good reference from the branch, despite having over-sprinkled her way to a legal ruckus.

The case came to a close at the end of 2012, with McDonald's releasing a statement that read: 'This matter has now been resolved to the satisfaction of both parties. The Employment Tribunal case has been withdrawn. No admission of liability was made.' In other words: 'We ran scared in the other direction when we realised one of our employees was actually able to understand they had rights.'

Perhaps, though, Carmarthen McDonald's should consider themselves lucky. In 2015 an employee across the pond, in Minnesota in the United States, had the most epic tantrum imaginable when he was fired by his manager. The shouting, swearing, screaming man was filmed ranting about the paucity of his wages and throwing food, drink and assorted items onto the floor of the restaurant in a video that was later uploaded and shared across the internet. He walked out of the door leaving an impressive trail of destruction behind him after eventually obeying orders to leave. Clearly, despite commercial claims to contrary, this guy was definitely not lovin' it.

SO WHAT CAN I DO?

So what rights do you have if you're fired from your casual Saturday job by a trigger-happy manager who thinks your over-sprinkling habits have gone too far? What counts as a sackable offence, and what counts as just plain stupid? And is it really advisable to err on the side of caution and to never pull your friend an extra-large pint or chuck them a bigger packet of chips, in case your manager comes out and sacks you on the spot?

- Everyone in employment has certain rights under the law. These include the right to claim compensation if unfairly dismissed. In most cases, to be able to claim unfair dismissal you will have to have worked for your employer for one year (if you started before 6 April 2012) or two years if you started on or after that date.

- You might have extra rights set out in your contract of employment. Read through this carefully, and see what it says about dismissal.

- If you are an agency worker, self-employed, a freelancer or a casual worker, these statutory rights might not apply to you, and you might not be able to make a claim for unfair dismissal. If you are being paid 'cash in hand' and you are aware that you are not paying tax or National Insurance contributions, then you are working illegally, and won't be able to rely on any law if you are unfairly dismissed.

What actually counts as dismissal?

- It does not have to be a straightforward 'you're fired'. Dismissal includes your employer ending your employment with or without notice, your employer not renewing a fixed-term contract, redundancy, your employer refusing to take you back after a strike or maternity leave, being forced to resign under pressure from your employer or being constructively dismissed. The last of these means your employer has made it impossible for you to carry on working so you have resigned.

- You may feel you have been dismissed because of your age, disability, gender reassignment, marriage or civil partnership, pregnancy and maternity, race, religion or belief, sex or sexual orientation. You can make a claim for discrimination to an employment tribunal instead of, or in addition to, a claim for unfair dismissal.

- You cannot be forced to retire just because you have reached a particular age, unless your employer can justify it. If they cannot, then you may have a claim for unfair dismissal under age discrimination. (However, this law changed in 2011. If you were 65 before 2011 and your employer forced you to retire, you can't claim for unfair dismissal.)

- If you have been dismissed, your employer usually should follow a proper dismissal and disciplinary procedure. They should send you a written statement, explaining why they want to fire you, and then organise a meeting with you to discuss the matter. If you want to appeal against your dismissal, you should be able to. This should be done in writing and within a reasonable time. You should also be entitled to a period of notice. If nothing is written about a notice period in your contract, then the employer has to give you a 'reasonable' notice. After the meeting or the appeal, they should give you their final decision. Your employer *should* follow this procedure, as set out in the Acas Code of Practice (you can find a link to the Acas website at the end of this book), but – just so you know – they do not have to. However, if you do proceed to an employment tribunal and your employer loses, they may be ordered to pay more compensation to you for not following the procedure. So, all of you employers out there, listen up and follow the procedure!

• As always, keep good records of everything that is said and done.

• If you think your employer's decision was unfair, you may be able to take your case to an employment tribunal or go through mediation.

Mediation

• Going through mediation is completely confidential and voluntary. The mediator will be impartial and independent and will facilitate communication between you and your employer. They might be already within your organisation or they might be an external mediator, specially brought in. This is unlikely to be free, but it should be the employer who pays and not you. The aim is to come to a solution that is acceptable to everyone. Of course, this might not happen.

The employment tribunal

- If you are not happy with the solution the mediator suggests, or you decided not to go for mediation at all, you can take your case to an employment tribunal. Do not jump straight into this decision as soon as you hear the words (Lord Sugar-style) 'You're fired!' Check your contract and make sure all of the steps of your particular employer's dismissal procedure have been followed. You might get a reduced award from the tribunal if you have jumped the gun. For example, if you are given the opportunity to appeal and you don't, any award you might get if you win may be reduced.

- However, there are strict time limits if you want to bring your case to an employment tribunal. The time limit is three months minus one day from the date of dismissal. This applies even if you appeal to your employer. But if you work out your notice, the date of the dismissal is when you stop working out your notice.

- If you are not sure whether you have a claim or not, you can seek advice from the Citizens Advice Bureau. If you are a member of a trade union, you can also speak to them to see what they can advise. Because of the time limit, it is incredibly important you seek advice as soon as you can. Deadlines will, in most cases, not be extended.

- Sometimes you might not be sure whether you were actually dismissed or not; for example, things get a bit heated and your boss shouts, 'Get out, I'm sick of the sight of you!' Not only is your boss a bit mean, he has also been pretty unclear. Seek advice.

- If your work keeps being given to other members of your team, and you are being shut out, this could amount to constructive dismissal. Seek advice. I know that you may be extremely stressed by the situation, but not as stressed as you will be when you realise the deadline has passed, and you are left with no job and no compensation and there is nothing you can do about it.

- Sarah was probably fired because of alleged misconduct. Dismissal for certain types of gross misconduct will likely be viewed as fair – harassment, theft, violence at work, not adhering to health and safety. Other types of behaviour which could be classed as misconduct could include being continuously late, carelessness, rudeness, not listening to instructions, and, of course, liberal use of sprinkles. The fairness of the dismissal in cases like this will depend on the circumstances. A person who swears at their manager once in the heat of the moment might not be fairly dismissed for their conduct, but someone whose language is 50 shades of blue when talking to customers and colleagues and who is consistently aggressive and insolent might be deemed to have deserved to be fired.

Do I need representation at the tribunal?

- The tribunal will look at evidence from both sides to decide whether your dismissal was unfair. Remember, while you may think giving your friend a little extra is harmless, someone is losing money somewhere and a judge may just consider what you did reprehensible.

You are not automatically entitled to representation if you do proceed to launch a claim, but in fact the system is set up so that you should be able to represent yourself. The tribunal is more informal than other courts, but it is still a legal process. If you do want someone to represent you, there are a few options.

1. You might have insurance to cover the cost of a solicitor, or be able to instruct a solicitor on a 'no win, no fee' basis.

2. Some CAB offices can offer not only advice, but also representation. In England and Wales there is no legal aid available for employment cases unless there is an issue with discrimination, which means you must feel you have been treated differently on account of your race, gender, age, religion, disability etc. In Scotland, you may be able to get free professional advice and assistance from a solicitor under the legal aid scheme. In special circumstances, you may also be able to get help towards legal representation. It will depend on your financial circumstances.

3. For information about other places where you can obtain free advice, go to the list I have provided at the end of this book.

• You must notify Acas (Advisory, Conciliation and Arbitration Service) before you make an application to the employment tribunal (either online or by phone). Employers and employees can take part in a free 'early conciliation' process, overseen by Acas, to see if legal proceedings can be averted. You will be asked if you want to participate, and then Acas will ask your employer. The process will be facilitated by Acas and will be much like mediation in that an independent conciliator will try to help you both come to a solution. If the claim is settled, Acas will prepare an agreement for you both to sign. If you do not resolve the dispute, or either party refuses to enter into the early conciliation process, you will be given an early conciliation certificate to show to the tribunal. Even if you know you do not want to enter conciliation, you still have to notify Acas. The three-month time limit is suspended while this process is ongoing.

- Recently, changes were made and it now costs up to £1,200 to bring a claim to an employment tribunal. However, if you are getting certain benefits or you are on a low monthly income, you may not have to pay all the fees. This is called a 'fee remission'. If you have to pay some or all of the fees, you can try to claim the costs back from your employer if you win.

- Studies have shown that the fee has seriously limited the amount of claims that are being brought. The aim was to stop 'vexatious' or bonkers claims, but in reality the chances are that many people who have valid claims which would have been successful just can't afford the risk and the money.

- In many cases people are not seeking huge amounts of money. Most just want the money they are owed, an apology, the reassurance that what happened to them won't happen to someone else, or, like Sarah above, a decent reference. Often the money that you will have to pay is wholly disproportionate to what you want from your ex-employer. It's not particularly fair, but you are going to have to seriously consider whether the benefits will outweigh the risks. Have a good look at your evidence, and consider what evidence your employer may have.

- Your adviser or representative will advise you on how strong or weak your case is and your likelihood of success. Of course, there is no guarantee. Always bear this in mind. Also consider whether your employer actually has enough money to pay you the compensation if you do win. Often employers can't afford to pay up, and the employee is left out of pocket.

How to make a claim at the employment tribunal

- Firstly (after you have contacted Acas and got the early conciliation certificate), you need to fill in the application form, called an ET1. You can get this online at www.justice.gov.uk on the Employment Tribunals page.

- On this form you will write a clear account of what happened and why you think it was unfair. Try to be concise, and write about the things that happened in the order they occurred. If you have an adviser or a representative, ask them for help filling this out.

- Your ET1 form needs to have arrived at the tribunal office by the time limit. In England and Wales, check www.justice.gov.uk for which office you should send the form to.

- You should get a Notice of Acknowledgement soon after you send in your ET1. If you do not, make sure you check with the tribunal before the time limit is up and resend it. The tribunal will copy your ET1 and send it to your employer to see if they want to respond or defend themselves. The tribunal will send you a copy of their response to you, roughly four weeks after you sent in your ET1 form.

- You might have to wait a long time for your hearing date, possibly six months or longer if it is a complicated case.

- At the hearing, you will have to make an affirmation or swear an oath before you present your evidence and you will be asked questions by the judge, your employer and possibly two other tribunal members.

- You will be sent the decision in the post a few days or weeks after the hearing. In certain cases you may also be given the decision at the hearing.

- You are very unlikely to have to pay your employer's costs if you lose. If you do, it's likely to be because you behaved badly during the running of the case, you refused a good settlement offer, or you should really not have brought the claim in the first place. MAKE SURE THIS DOES NOT APPLY TO YOU!

Kirk's case – terrible tattoos

The problem with inking anything permanent on your skin is that it might end up totally irrelevant, slightly embarrassing, or just plain outdated in the years to come, while your skin remains steadfastly attached to your body. You may have toyed with the idea of getting 'TAYLOR 4EVER' emblazoned across your chest in a feat of college passion, or thought briefly that a Mexican drinking worm might be a good idea. If you remember on one memorable occasion in my courtroom, one particularly stupid gentleman agreed with his genius of a friend to have a tattoo of a penis on his leg. Think that was bad? Listen to what Kirk Soccorso did!

Kirk was a romantic lad with an interest in getting tats in hidden places (no, I don't mean there!) Four years before, when he was still with his ex-girlfriend, he'd made the eternal mistake of getting her name tattooed on himself – but, Never fear, he thought. It's in a place that nobody would guess, and what could possibly be offensive about a beautiful young girl's name anyway?

What turned out to be the nail in the coffin of Kirk's career was not actually the placement of the tattoo, however, but what it said. Now, when he decided to show off his ink to his fellow employees, it was the beginning of 2015, when news about the Islamic State of Iraq and Syria was in full swing. Inhumane torture, massacres and beheadings were being routinely reported in the news. Kirk, who worked as a tool demonstrator in New York (and yes, I can think of many uses for that job title as well, but we're all mature adults here and we're not going to mention them), overheard one of his colleagues talking about the latest atrocity. Having heard only a few words, he marched over and thought he'd found the perfect moment to whip out the tattoo in question. And so he did, pulling down his tongue to reveal a clear word on the inside of his mouth; in large black letters, the tattoo read 'ISIS'.

Just like the girl whose Australian parents complained to the media that their daughter Isis was getting a bit of a hard time at kindergarten after the extremist terrorist group kept hogging more column inches than the toddler's latest creation out of Play-Doh, Kirk's ex-girlfriend had been so called after the Egyptian goddess of nature. It probably seemed like a wonderful and unique idea at the time, but now I think it's fair to say that Islamic State has ruined the name for all of us, along with the less important concepts of human dignity and Western perceptions of the Muslim faith. This backstory wasn't immediately available to Kirk's colleagues at the New York Home Depot, however. All they saw and heard was a conversation about the latest beheadings by ISIS, followed by a man who had 'ISIS' tattooed on the inside of his mouth. It's not an everyday occurrence.

Soccorso, who had been working at the store for six months, was let go from his position after the inking proved a step too far for his understandably sensitive co-workers. However, when the bizarre case hit the media, his employers claimed that it wasn't 'just the tattoo' that contributed to his dismissal, and stuck to their guns. Meanwhile, Kirk claimed that he wasn't a news-follower and hadn't known the significance of ISIS when he'd moseyed on over to show off his unfortunate choice in body art, and that he was a victim of mistaken anger, as well as his own stupidity. Honestly, he'd just thought they were chatting about a girl who shared his ex's name. Perhaps the fact that he couldn't even keep up with even the most basic of current events contributed to his boss's reservations about trusting him around sharp tools at any time in the future!

SO WHAT CAN I DO?

If you have some interesting body ink adorning your skin, what can you expect from an employer? Are they within their rights to hire, fire or demand cover-ups from you if they take a dislike to what you've etched on yourself, even if the tattoo in question doesn't quite make it seem like you're supporting a well-known terrorist organisation? And if you do suspect that you've been fired for appearance alone, but your boss tries to get around it by claiming that you were also a bad employee, will an employment tribunal look upon you sympathetically? Or should you just consign yourself and your Grumpy Cat forehead tattoo to the career dustbin?

Under the Equality Act 2010, tattoos, body art and piercings are not protected characteristics and in respect of disability discrimination, tattoos are expressly stated as not amounting to a disability. Therefore, there is no separate cause of action of 'visible tattoo my boss doesn't really like, so he has sacked me'.

However, as I have mentioned above, an employee cannot be dismissed unfairly. Unfairness might include dismissing an employee for a tattoo. The judge will look at the circumstances, and may well find that the employee was unfairly dismissed.

Some occupations are more likely to already have tattoo policies. The Metropolitan Police has forbidden police from getting visible tattoos, stating that they 'damage the professional image' of the force. If you are starting a new job, be sure to find out if your employers have any policies regarding tattoos. An employer is well within their rights to have such a policy. However, if you are already employed and your company decides to implement a tattoo policy, they are likely to offer some kind of flexibility. If you are an employer and you are thinking of implementing such a policy, consider your current staff. It's not as if you can ask them to remove their tattoos. (Can you imagine removing a mouth tattoo, even if it does appear to profess your allegiance to some really not very nice people? The pain!) Be very clear about your policy. Will you only prohibit certain tattoos? What area of the body counts as being visible? When we get one of our few sunny days, and we collectively unleash our pasty white skin on the world, will you prohibit a tiny tattoo on an employee's shoulder? Will you only implement the policy for customer-facing employees?

Thinking about all these issues and ensuring your employees know the score may save you a headache down the line when your best, most loyal employee gets an 'I heart [insert company name here]' face tattoo.

SOCIAL MEDIA AT WORK

Increasingly the lines between our personal and professional lives are becoming blurred. Often work does not finish when you leave the revolving doors of the office at 6pm. Many people spend hours and hours on their iPhone. This results in the line between work and home getting dangerously blurred.

The problem with social media is that once something is out there, you cannot take it back. There are no safeguards. Within moments, your tweet could be twittering all over the world and before you know it, you've gone viral with a trending hashtag to prove it.

James's case

Social media is a fickle thing, prone to throwing up photos of your ex getting with their new beau (a model, of course) while you're walking across high bridges, or openly identifying what you're really doing when you're 'working in your room' with an accidental copy-and-paste Twitter accident (let's never forget when the delightfully named US politician Anthony Weiner posted a particularly saucy photo of his member which ended up publicly viewable on the social network). Just how far you can go with your Twitter, your Facebook and your Instagram in the modern career world always seems to be a matter of debate. But one supermarket has made it very clear that they have a zero-tolerance attitude towards insults from their employees on the big, bad internet, and you can be sure it ain't Lidl. Nope, the trail is being blazed by than none other than our very own badasses of kale and quinoa, Waitrose.

Now, you might have the impression that Waitrose wouldn't be that hard on the people it employs to stand behind its artisanal cheese counters and give out free teas and coffees at the on-horse drive-through to members of the aristocracy. Not so, however – just because their soufflés are as soft as if they'd been concocted by angels, that doesn't mean that this store for the aspirational classes is soft on its workers. This was found out the hard way by one young man, 20-year-old James Brennan, who was fired from his job for making a slur about Waitrose and its associates on his Facebook page after coming home from a particularly difficult day at work at one of its central London stores. What did he write in the offending post? 'F*ck the Partnership' – meaning, of course, the John Lewis Partnership that owns Waitrose alongside its other chains.

One of his more assiduous fellow employees spotted that James had strayed from Big Brother's benevolent eye and taken it upon himself to express an individual view about the company that he worked for. The employee in question went on to James's Facebook page, screenshotted the offending post and printed it out to show to managerial staff. Needless to say, once managers had seen that James had disrespected the Partnership, they knew he had to go.

'At the end of the day, what I wrote was private,' James told the media after he was unceremoniously fired. 'You would never get sacked for saying something like that in the pub. I was sacked from Waitrose for something I said on Facebook in my own time. . . It is an infringement of my privacy.'

So where does the law stand on new issues like this? Is everything you write on social media – even if, as in James's case, it was made private and only seeable by Facebook friends – considered sufficiently within the public domain to warrant a firing if you step out of line? Is anything you post on the internet safe? And is there any way to challenge a big corporation if they demand complete online loyalty from you across all your social networks, or does freedom of speech not apply in the cybersphere the way that it might in conversations over a pint in real life?

RINDER'S RULES

- A sensible employer, if they are down with the kids and up with the times, should have a social-media policy. This should state what the employer deems as acceptable use by employees and can include, if they wish, what employees post in their personal time.

It should state whether the employer intends to actively monitor their employee's social media.

- If disciplinary action or a dismissal arises out of something that has been posted on social media, the employer must still follow their procedures as set out in employee contracts, and should follow the Acas guidelines. Any disciplinary action should be proportionate.

- Under human-rights law, everyone has freedom of expression and this is a right that the courts will protect. Any action taken by the employer will be weighed up against the employee's right to their freedom of expression.

- The employer has to have acted reasonably and fairly for the tribunal to uphold their decision. The court will consider whether what was said was mild or strongly offensive, and look at what actual harm has been caused to the company.

- You may say that what you write on your own Facebook page is yours and you deserve the right to privacy, particularly if you have strong privacy settings that allow only your friends to see your posts. This does not matter. A post can be screenshotted or forwarded, and some people have thousands of friends (who I am sure are all very, very close friends).

- If your employer does not have a social-media policy, they might find it pretty difficult to enforce appropriate use by their employees, or launch disciplinary or dismissal proceedings after an offending post has been made. However, whether they will succeed in defending a claim for unfair dismissal at an employment tribunal will again depend on what exactly the post says and the impact it will have on the company. *So think before you tweet!*

- Always assume that prospective employers will be looking at what you put on Facebook, Instagram, Twitter and the next newfangled social media mega-company on the block. Use a pseudonym, change your privacy settings, just don't let your potential future boss see pictures of you drunk. Employers aren't supposed to discriminate by judging from appearances, but if you wouldn't turn up to an interview like that, why would you broadcast it for the world to see? First impressions count.

THEFT AT WORK –
HOW ILLEGAL IS IT?

The Crown Prosecution Service has discretion when deciding whether to pursue charges against someone, and one of the factors they will take into account is whether it's in the public interest to do so. Depending on the circumstances, they might decide that a person did not have any dishonest intentions and that it would waste everyone's time and money by going to court. On the other hand, the CPS would be well within their rights to charge, because a law has been broken. Your good intentions may be hard to prove, and I wouldn't push your luck. Your employer might not be quite as charitable as Goodwill were with Andrew – read on.

Stealing is stealing, whether it's to fund something frivolous or to do good.

Robin Hood and the eventual court case – Andrew's do-gooding

Nineteen-year-old Andrew Anderson was working at a store in Florida when he realised that a lot of the customers who came in to buy things looked pretty poor. The ones who were struggling were easy to see: they turned up on broken-down bicycles rather than in cars, they were wearing layers of clothes because everything they owned was on their backs, and they'd come in without wallets, clutching two or three dollars in their dirty hands, because they had nothing else in the world but were hoping for a bargain. This was in part unsurprising, because Goodwill is essentially a chain of charity shops in America. Its ethos is to take discarded items, update them and then sell them in thrift stores across the country, and it also prides itself on employing people with disabilities, veterans, those with little or no education, and those facing severe employment difficulties. It describes itself as a 'unique enterprise' that 'defies traditional distinctions' on 'people, planet and performance' in the retail world. But that doesn't mean that it takes have-a-go Robin Hood efforts lightly, as Andrew was about to find out.

Andrew had a big heart, and he was touched by what he saw while working at the Goodwill shop in Florida. Every now and then, when someone came in who looked like they were finding it particularly hard to make ends meet, he would give them a discount that allowed them to walk away with the items they needed. A ten-dollar kettle might magically become a four-dollar kettle if that person only had ten with them and desperately needed baby clothes as well. A sturdy winter coat and a pair of boots might end up with 50 per cent off at Andrew's till if it was clear that the person didn't have a functioning place to go home to after they left the safety of the store.

After a few months of this happening, however, the Goodwill managers caught on. The money just wasn't adding up, and items seemed to have mysteriously gone without the price being settled. Once they figured out that everything was happening on Andrew's shift, the situation seemed to become clear. Believing him to have pocketed the cash himself, his bosses reported him to Collier County police, and Andrew was arrested.

THE VERDICT

Luckily for Andrew, he didn't end up with a criminal record at the end of the day. The police and the other Goodwill employees did their investigations and estimated that he had cheated the store out of approximately $4,000 – but there was absolutely no evidence that he had ever had the money himself. It turned out that he really had just been exercising his own goodwill, albeit somewhat misguidedly.

'Goodwill is a helping and giving company, so I took it upon myself to be giving and helping because I feel people deserve it,' the boy told NBC2 when interviewed. What he lacked in business knowledge, he made up for in kind intentions.

Realising at this point that failing to exercise *their* goodwill when dealing with the big-hearted Andrew Anderson might slightly damage public perceptions of their business, Goodwill backed down and agreed not to press charges for theft. Stealing is still against the values of the organisation, they said, and so Andrew would remain jobless – but they wouldn't take him to court, since he hadn't done the usual teenager thing and blown it all on something to impress a girl at college. He got away with a firing and a tiny bit of grudging respect. His bosses admitted that had they known the circumstances of his messing with the finances, then they probably never would have involved the police at all.

SO WHAT CAN I DO?

Are people in the UK as likely to get away with fiddling the till if it turns out that they did it for philanthropic reasons? Can you prove your intentions anyway? Would Goodwill have had a solid case for taking Andrew to court and making him pay back the money if they had not decided to drop the charges – or does the law look more kindly upon people who give to grannies than those who just have themselves a radical weekend with cash they have rinsed from their Saturday job? And what should you do if you're faced with your very own give-to-the-poor situation, whether it's in a charity shop or a larger corporate environment?

RINDER'S RULES

- If you think you have been unfairly dismissed act quickly!

- There is lots of free advice out there to help you determine whether you want to pursue your claim.

Listen to what these people have to say. Despite what you may think, unless you were a city banker and have lost out on millions of pounds as a result of your employer's actions, you may not make a lot of money out of your case.

- Decide exactly what you want from your employer before you take action. Compensation? A reference? Money?

- Check your contract (assuming you have one) carefully and pay special attention to the discipline procedures, which should be easy to understand. Make sure, in the event that you end up in a situation like this at work, that your employer follows their procedures to the letter.

- Don't ever be intimidated by your employer! If they have acted unlawfully, be brave and do not let them get away with it. Remember, if they have treated you like this, then there is a good chance that others are also suffering.

LAWYERS!

There is a well-known joke which goes something like this: What do you call five thousand lawyers at the bottom of the sea? A start. (Yes, I know; it's hilarious!) In most cases this is entirely unfair. The overwhelming majority of lawyers I have worked alongside are deeply committed people and, since legal aid has been savagely cut, these men and women work tirelessly for very little reward. Let me be clear! There are no fat-cat barristers living off the public purse any more. Many junior barristers, particularly those who take publicly funded cases, make far less than the average national salary.

For the most part, this book deals with legal situations you may find yourself in where you could (and in most instances should) pursue a case in the small claims court yourself. I absolutely encourage you, where possible, to do that. In some circumstances, however, especially those cases which cannot be dealt with by the small claims court, it is always advisable to instruct a specialist lawyer. I know this can be expensive, but bringing complicated or high-value cases to court is incredibly demanding and hiring a lawyer will – I assure you – save you money in the long run. A person who opts for self-representation should remember the saying 'A man who is his own lawyer has a fool for a client.'

Although most lawyers are entirely professional, there are circumstances where solicitors and barristers are frankly useless: they make up fictional bills, they fail to do the work they promise, or show up at court looking like they've spent the night in a hedge and reek of booze. Although this situation is – happily – very rare, this chapter contains some of my favourite tales of those who have represented themselves (aka morons) and dodgy lawyers from around the world (including advice on what to do if you happen to have the misfortune of hiring one).

The case of Heather Mills: why representing yourself is inadvisable

We all have our favourite divorce cases – I know I do – and the one that really gets me going every time is the Mills–McCartney legal slanging match back in 2008. There's a celebrity, a large settlement and a lawyer nicknamed the Steel Magnolia: everything you could possibly need for good-quality entertainment. Who could ask for more?

When the Mills–McCartney marriage came to an end, Sir Paul wasn't messing around. He knew he was in danger of losing a large proportion of his fortune, and so he hired Fiona Shackleton – previously the lawyer for Prince Charles's divorce – to represent him.

Either way, Paul had a plan. His soon-to-be-ex-wife Heather had a plan too, and it was to bypass the lawyer route altogether. After all, in a legal situation where emotions run high and millions of pounds of your money is at stake, who needs a middleman? Why not just go ahead and represent yourself? It seemed like an excellent idea at the time.

Ever the level-headed player, Heather really outdid herself during this case. When the judge's final decision was handed down, leaving her with a £25-million settlement that translates to more than £700 for every hour that she was married to Paul (plus £35,000 per year for her daughter Beatrice's private school fees and other assorted assets), she was less than impressed. Incensed by the perceived unfairness of the deal, Heather took it upon herself to communicate her distaste through the medium of liquid, and promptly poured a jug of water over the head of her husband's lawyer. She then cackled loudly and declared that Shackleton had been 'baptised in court', quite literally adding insult to injury.

Now, many of us may sympathise with the actions of Ms Mills here. After all, there are at least a handful of people I've encountered in my life who I genuinely believe I should have been paid far more than £700 an hour to endure. However, at that point I made the classic error of failing to marry a millionaire, falling at the hurdle so many others have fallen at before me. Heather, however, had done her homework – and she believed that she deserved at least a little bit more of the £125-million settlement she'd been gunning for. She'd put in the time and the effort, for God's sake. Where was the pay-off?

THE VERDICT

Unfortunately, the court disagreed. Fiona Shackleton, far more experienced in disputes such as these and substantially less emotionally involved with the case at hand, remained tight-lipped and refused to speak to the media. Heather decided otherwise, and minutes after accusing Fiona of 'letting down womankind' by representing men in the courtroom, she ran out onto the front steps of the court and delivered an impressive tirade against Fiona, lawyers and the entire legal system of the UK in a speech that lasted 12 minutes. Meanwhile, we all wept for her impending poverty.

Both Heather and Paul had agreed during their divorce that neither would reveal specific details to the media without obtaining consent from the other. It didn't really work out that way. And matters usually remain private when they go through the Family Court, but Paul had wanted financial details to be discussed in the open, apparently so that nobody could accuse him of short-changing his ex. Heather rolled her eyes at the decision and suggested that her ex-husband just wanted to be seen by the British public as 'the generous Sir Paul'.

Whatever the exact details of the ongoing quarrel, one thing was crystal clear: Heather had it in for her husband's lawyer. She and Fiona had never quite seen eye to eye, even before the baptism incident. Heather believed that, when she turned up to one legal meeting in a wheelchair, Fiona had told people she was trying it on for a bit of the old disability sympathy. And, according to Mills, Shackleton had called her 'many, many names' during the legal negotiations that led up to the court case. What went on behind closed doors is only for a select group of people to know, but Mills felt so strongly about it that she ended up reporting Fiona Shackleton to the Law Society for professional misconduct. It's unlikely that Fiona went crying back to her office though, considering that she walked away with a substantial amount in legal fees from Sir Paul herself.

SO WHAT CAN I DO?

Heather sacked her original lawyers because they were charging too much and – she felt – she could do the job better herself. So if you really think your lawyer is charging too much, can or should you sue them? And is it truly illegal for a lawyer to call somebody names or tell them that their wheelchair is only for sympathy during meetings? What's the best outcome if you choose to retaliate by dousing their head in water at a courtroom session? Is taking issue with your ex-spouse's legal representative during a break-up going to be taken seriously by a court of law? See my Rinder's Rules at the end of this chapter!

LEGAL AFFAIRS – ARE THEY WORTH THE RISK?

So where does UK law stand on client–attorney relationships, and why? What happens if you also find your legal representative so incredibly irresistible that trysts happen outside (or inside) the courtroom? How common are these little errors, and how seriously are they seen by others if you're caught? And what happens to a legal professional who takes it too far – is their career over for good, or are human urges given a bit of leeway in the eyes of the law?

A *case of bad judgement*

It's always nice to feel like you've got a bit more than your money's worth – but every now and then, this can backfire spectacularly. Here's one tale that will have you questioning whether a little extra thrown in is really worth the hassle.

Lisa Traylor-Wolff was a well-respected senior judge working in Indiana in the US across two counties. She'd seen her fair share of cases and handed down harsh but fair judgments on those who had strayed in society. In her middle age, she knew the lie of the land and she knew the law inside out. She had a reputation to protect, a career to uphold and a wealth of experience in dealing with clients. Lisa was a pro.

But it turned out that Lisa had a bit of a sneaky side. When she wasn't working on her usual cases as a senior judge, she also part-timed in two important roles: defence lawyer and serial dater.

How do we know this? Because Lisa, hopped up on the undeniably aphrodisiac qualities of the legal system, met up with one of her 26-year-old clients one day and decided she was going to service him in more ways than one. So what if he'd been in a spot of trouble in the past?

There are those of you who might think that a lawyer getting romantically involved with her client could affect the objectivity of her judgement, and that's pretty much how US law and most other legal systems see it too. Things could have turned into a full-scale scandal if Lisa's client had been acquitted of his crimes in the courtroom, but funnily enough, it seemed that she hadn't been paying enough attention to the job in hand (no laughter, please, we're not animals). The toy boy was convicted of his crimes and sent to prison at the Miami Correctional Facility in Peru, Indiana. Talk about banged up.

Many would assume that the love affair ended at this point – but not so. In what seems like a set-up for a rather saucy movie, but actually happened in real life, Lisa went to visit her lover – still posing as his attorney, arriving to give him legal advice on appealing his sentence – and ended up giving him a whole lot more, in a meeting area for clients and lawyers at the prison itself. Needless to say, everyone became a little bit suspicious of how enthusiastically the young man was receiving his legal advice and the couple were caught in a very compromising position in the interview room. 'I'm just fixing Mummy's back' might work when your kids walk in on an awkward situation, but there's no easy go-to excuse for when a group of police officers find themselves suddenly involved with your re-enactment of cheap video erotica at the county jail.

THE VERDICT

Needless to say, Lisa wasn't looked upon too kindly by the rest of her profession. She was formally accused of violating four rules of professional conduct for defence lawyers, as well as undermining her independence, integrity and impartiality as a judge. She didn't ask for her judgeship to be renewed, which was probably a good call, but there's no word on whether her enthusiasm for young tearaways half her age has been quelled.

LAWYER INCOMPETENCY

So how much do you have to take from a lawyer before you have grounds for an official complaint? Can you halt a court process if it's pretty obvious that the man is taking naps rather than working up a good legal defence? Is there the option in the UK to reverse a decision after conviction if your lawyer really was that bad? And do you get a choice, if your incompetent legal representation was supplied by the state rather than chosen by you? Read on to find out!

Asleep on the job

You may think that Lisa did her young client no favours by encouraging him to take off his pants in the interview room, but there are some lawyers who have been so monumentally useless that they could leave you craving a 'cougar' (I discovered what this meant in a recent case I sat on). Take Texas lawyer Martin Zimmerman, for instance, who was openly branded 'the worst lawyer ever' in the American media in 2013 after his client – who was convicted for drink-driving with a child in the car and spitting on a police officer – complained that he had barely represented him in the courtroom.

Most of the time we might have reason to disbelieve what criminals are saying, especially if they're complaining that they went to prison because of an error on their lawyer's part rather than their own actions. However, this one seemed pretty reasonable. The defence attorney had, after all, introduced his client to the jury as Jonathan Dextor. Nothing unusual about that – apart from the fact that the man's name was actually Daniel Textor.

Having set the bar pretty low with that initial error, Zimmerman didn't exactly work to raise it. He slept through most of the trial, taking naps so frequently in court that he managed to completely overlook a plea bargain that would have worked in his client's favour. Textor was facing 60 months for spitting on the police officer and an additional 28 for driving drunk with a minor in the car, but had previously been offered a deal of 45 months for the former and 20 for the latter. Since Zimmerman had dozed off during the time available to submit the plea, Textor ended up with the much higher sentence. One catnap was costing a defendant 20 extra months in prison.

THE VERDICT

Luckily, when Textor made an official complaint about the incompetence of a man who didn't know his name and used most of his time in court to catch up on some Zs, he and his lawyer were given a chance to submit the missed plea bargain again. The assistant district attorney who heard the complaint was apparently 'sympathetic' with Zimmerman, who said that he had sleep apnoea and found it hard to control his napping tendencies. However, the DA did ultimately decide that Zimmerman shouldn't be paid the $4,400 from public funds that he would have been given for defending his client.

'There's no reason the taxpayers should pay him for not doing his job,' he was quoted as saying, having clearly never visited any public-sector workplaces in the UK. And we all do have to agree with him, considering that some defence lawyers like Lisa Traylor-Wolff are going above and beyond the call of duty. In the end, however, nobody's going to look kindly on doing anything in a legal setting which should be reserved for either the bedroom or perhaps a very deserted beach if you have a lot of towels. Whether you're sleeping with your client or beside him, it's never a good look.

A LAWYER'S REPUTATION – WHAT TO LOOK OUT FOR

We're all game for a bit of entertainment in the courtroom, but when do the efforts of a lawyer to laugh you out of a conviction go too far? Is it really legally unacceptable to promote the idea that your defence attorney can get you out of being sentenced to prison, even when you committed the crime you're accused of? And what exactly are the restrictions placed on the lawyer–client relationship: can a criminal confide that they actually did do the deed, when their lawyer is presenting a case to the courtroom that depends on them believing their client is innocent? Is the lawyer duty-bound to tell the judge if their client has made a confidential confession? Can you really build your career on getting people out of prison who may well be a danger to the community?

Rapping it up

Finally, there is the case of one man who has one of the most unusual CVs an employer could hope to come across. Thirty-one-year-old Daniel Muessig made headlines in 2014 after the 'rapper-turned-lawyer' (yes, rapper-turned-lawyer) came out with a bunch of controversial commercials on YouTube advertising his services to criminals. He claimed that he had had a 'quarter-life crisis' after spending the preceding decade in freestyle rap, and decided to qualify as a criminal attorney to get over it, graduating from the University of Pittsburgh School of Law in 2012. Clearly the mid-life crisis, with its legal 'babes' adorning your new soft-top sports car as you drive off into the sunset with only a small suitcase, your divorce papers and the echoes of your children's cries to 'come back, Daddy, please' as fading memories of your thirties is falling out of vogue. Case studies and juries are the champagne and Ferraris of the quarter-life-crisis world.

There aren't that many people who enter the legal profession from the underground musical sphere; my own short-lived career in rap was never built to last. Daniel, then, was something of a unique specimen. So once he qualified, Dan knew that he wasn't going to just sit back and do things the way they'd been done for so many years before. He was going to shake up the legal profession with his innovative new ideas and the 'improvisational arguments' he'd learnt from rap (his words, not mine). He realised that he needed a novel way of pulling in the clients. And that's when YouTube came to mind.

In the three-and-a-half-minute-long video that Daniel ended up creating, he made it clear that he was fairly open to clientele who definitely had committed their crimes and needed a slick legal representative to wrangle them out of it. In one clip, a man dressed as a burglar climbed out of a window holding a stolen laptop, as the words 'Crimes Committed: Burglary, Prescription Fraud, Receiving Stolen Property' flashed up on-screen. 'Thanks, Dan!' the burglar said with a grin, doing the thumbs-up sign to the camera. Inspiring!

Elsewhere, a man wearing a balaclava and photocopying a dollar bill said a muffled 'Thanks, Dan!' while the screen informed the viewer that he had committed 'Conspiracy', and in another scene, a man wearing a sweatshirt that said 'HUSTLE GANG' was shown selling drugs and thanking Dan for getting him out of prison. It was certainly a new and creative take on legal advertising, but surprisingly, Muessig's local bar association were less than supportive. A spokesman said that the commercial was 'an insult to lawyers across the country, who take great pride in their profession'. He was slightly worried that people who had committed crimes might watch the advert and think that 'if you commit a crime this attorney will get you off without any explanation'.

What are the legal duties of my lawyer?

Are all solicitors or barristers money-grabbing, incompetent philanderers, who are willing to provide a false alibi or fabricate a defence on your behalf? The answer is unequivocally no. Of course, the profession I love has had (and I am sure always will have) those who let it down; in the same way, honest traders, the medical profession or the police sometimes have the odd bad egg.

In the UK the conduct of solicitors and barristers is regulated by the Solicitors Regulation Authority (SRA) or the Bar Standards Board (BSB). Barristers and solicitors must act in the best interests of their clients, not compromise their independence and not act in any way which would lower the public trust in the legal profession.

They can be – and sometimes are – held strictly to account when they break those rules. The penalties can also be severe.

There is something called legal privilege which is an extremely important legal principle. It means that whatever you tell your lawyer is confidential. They cannot blurt out in court what you have told them in your meetings, unless you expressly tell them they can.

So can you tell your lawyer you are guilty of a criminal offence? You can, and if you want to plead not guilty, they can and must continue to represent you. However, other than speaking on your behalf at your sentencing hearing they could never continue to act for you at the trial. They could not, for example, make an impassioned speech to the jury declaring your innocence. I am often asked about this at parties (usually by thoroughly unimaginative bores). How can you represent someone when you know they're guilty? The answer is simple.

I don't! If a defendant in a criminal case claims that they are innocent then it is my job (and the job of all lawyers) to advance the defendant's case. Nothing more! If a defendant tells me that they are guilty I would, in every possible likelihood, withdraw from the case.

Solicitors and barristers must:

1. give you advice that is in your best interests.
2. treat you fairly
3. give you all the information you need so you can decide about the services you need
4. tell you how your problem will be handled and the options available to you
5. tell you about your right to complain and how to make a complaint
6. give you information about costs

It is a big step for most people to seek to employ the services of a solicitor. It is more often than not a very stressful time in their lives.

What should my lawyer do for me?

- Lawyers need to give you options of how you could proceed. Examples for civil cases could include: doing nothing; going through mediation; attending a Citizens Advice Bureau; or – best of all – advising you to go to a small claims court yourself.

- Although criminal procedures are different, the guiding principles are the same. The solicitor or barrister should listen and advise you of the options open to you based on what you have told them.

- *This is the really important thing!* Your lawyer must from the start explain the cost implications. Legal representation is not cheap; you are not just paying for their time but also for the upkeep of the building they work in, support staff and expenses incurred. You will be charged for meetings, emails, phone calls, letters, conferences, photocopying, preparation time (and, yes, this may even include thinking) in addition to all court appearances.

- Your lawyer should explain their fee, usually expressed as cost per hour or a fixed fee for the whole case. They should discuss other funding arrangements, such as 'no win, no fee', and explore whether you have legal expenses insurance cover and whether financial assistance, such as legal aid, may be available to you.

- Charges vary between different lawyers and law firms and it may therefore be in your interests to shop around, as the next solicitor in the high street may charge less. However, sometimes you get what you pay for, so ensure you weigh up cost against quality. Research and recommendation is invaluable. You can go on the SRA or the BSB website and check whether they are registered, what they specialise in, and whether they have had any disciplinary action against them.

- Your legal adviser should tell you whether a barrister is likely to be needed and what their fees might be, and be realistic in setting out how many thousands of pounds could be involved, assessing the likelihood of success but (and here is the important thing) pointing out that there is no real guarantee that you will win. They should also explain in civil cases that if you lose, this may result in your paying costs to the other side, including their legal fees.

You may see your lawyer taking copious notes when they are with you so that they can retrieve your instructions at any stage, reminding them what was agreed. You need to keep similar timed and dated notes of all contact, or attempted contact, with the lawyer. If things go awry later those records may greatly assist you. Do not just start keeping records when it starts to look like something is going wrong: *keep them from the beginning*.

SO WHAT CAN I DO?

Things can go wrong. Relationships between the lawyer and client can deteriorate. Reasons for the discontent can be many: a breakdown of communication; the needy client contacting the lawyer too often; the lawyer who doesn't answer telephone calls. Some things can be fixed, but others (such as a lawyer losing original documentation or missing a court appearance or a legal deadline) can have legal implications that are not reversible and must be dealt with.

You must first try to resolve the complaint by discussing it with your legal adviser. If this does not work you need to use their company's complaints procedure. All law firms must have a written complaints procedure and the firm will tell you who to contact if you have a problem with the legal adviser handling your case. The legal adviser must give you a copy of the complaints procedure if you ask for it. Usually you will be told to put the complaint in a letter. If it's a solicitor's firm, there will typically be a complaints-handling partner. If your complaint is against a barrister, address your complaint to the barrister themselves.

The website of the Legal Ombudsman helpfully has a template of a complaint letter you can use at www.legal ombudsman.org.uk.

If this does not resolve the matter or there has been no response within eight weeks, you should contact the Legal Ombudsman. This is a free and impartial service that can help you with complaints against solicitors, barristers and other legal professionals. You must contact them within six months of the firm's response (assuming they responded in the first place) and within six years of the complaint arising or three years of your becoming aware of the need for a complaint.

You can also call their helpline number if you want to actually speak to someone!

What does the Legal Ombudsman do?

They will first ask you to send them the complaint letter you sent to your legal adviser, and any response that they made to you. This can be done online or by post. Never send any original documents, just copies, unless they ask specifically for originals. They will look at these and see if there is anything they can do to help you. If they can't help, they will signpost you to someone that might be able to. An investigator will look at your complaint and tell you whether you did receive poor service or not. If you did, the Legal Ombudsman will facilitate you and your firm working things out, but if that is not possible, they have official powers to resolve problems. They can make a decision, which will be final and binding. These decisions can include an apology from the legal adviser, a reduction in the legal fees that have been paid, or compensation for being treated badly or if you have lost out because of their poor service.

What they cannot do, however, is give you legal advice or represent you in legal proceedings. They do not look at negligence cases against legal providers. For these you will need to seek legal advice from another legal adviser. The Legal Ombudsman only deals with the level of customer service from the legal provider. Often a negligent lawyer will provide poor service, so there will be an overlap and it is up to you which course to take.

What if I want to sue my lawyer for negligence?

If your legal adviser has been negligent, you may be able to take legal action against them as well as making a complaint. You will need to get legal advice. The standard of care that is required of a lawyer (the test that the court will apply when considering whether or not they have been a complete shyster, in other words) is whether or not they have been reasonably competent. If your lawyer acted in a way which falls below this standard and you lost money as a direct result of mistakes that your lawyer made, then they are liable for damages.

Although you may feel let down by the legal profession as a whole (and the last thing you want to do is go back to another lawyer), you should ask for legal advice if you think you may have a negligence claim. Your new lawyer will be able to assess whether what happened to you amounted to an arguable case for negligence, or just poor service. Often you might be given a free introductory session, where they will see if you may have a case or not.

All solicitors and barristers have to have insurance against negligence claims, and if you do pursue a claim, the insurance companies will in all likelihood become involved. They may decide to try to settle your claim out of court, or proceed to court. It is likely to be a long process, but if you think you have a case then you have a responsibility to pursue it. Be brave!

CHAPTER 11

REPRESENTING YOURSELF: A GOOD IDEA?

If you have a claim that is eligible to proceed in the small claims court, then you can and should be able to represent yourself. The next chapter will tell you how to launch a claim in the small claims court in England and Wales and the sheriff court in Scotland.

If I have a case which is too big for the small claims court, should I proceed without the assistance of a lawyer?

The answer to this question is, in short, NO. Here's why.

- No one wants to pay for lawyers, especially when they have already lost money or are in a stressful and worrying situation. Legal fees can build up quickly and before you know it, you've spent hundreds or thousands of pounds.

- But you pay the fees and instruct a lawyer because you have to, right? There's no other choice. Nope, you can, in a lot of cases, represent yourself. This is called being a 'litigant in person'. You can be a litigant in person both in a civil claim and in a criminal case where you are the defendant. There are more and more litigants in person appearing in courts up and down the UK, as cuts to legal aid means more people cannot be represented for free.

- But just because you can, that doesn't mean that you should. The small claims court procedure has been developed to be quick and easy for non-lawyers to represent themselves. However, if your case is being heard in the small claims court and is particularly complex, or if the value of your claim is too high for the small claims court, you really should seek legal advice.

- Despite the pretty negative general view of lawyers, the vast majority are good at their jobs and have studied for many years to qualify. They have all spent three or four years at university, and have then taken a year's practical course. Then they will have spent a further two years as a trainee (for solicitors) or a year's pupillage (as a barrister). Competition for these jobs is so high nowadays that only the best get through, so even the young'uns are likely to be very good at what they do. And as for older lawyers, you just can't beat experience. You are most likely going to be facing your opponent's lawyer who has years and years of experience in the particular area of law you are dealing with, and you will be disadvantaged by this fact – you are highly unlikely to be able to reach their level of expertise in the time it takes to get to court. There will be allowances made for the fact that you are not represented by a lawyer – for example, the judge will take extra time to explain things to you – but that does not mean that your opponent's lawyer will be easy on you, or will jeopardise their client's case to help you out.

- Do not go into it thinking that it will be in any way easy. You will need to get to grips with not only the law surrounding your particular issue, but also all the procedure (which needs to be strictly followed). Your case can be dismissed or you can be penalised just by missing deadlines or not filing documents properly. It is a lawyer's job to know these procedures like the back of their hand.

- You will need to spend lots of time preparing your case and your documents, in addition to knowing the law and procedures. Consider whether you have the time to do all of this to the level that's required in order for you to win your case. Think about all the resources that are available to a lawyer, from legal assistants to access to legal books and online databases, and whether you working alone can measure up.

- A lawyer will know how to approach reaching a settlement before going to court, and how to get the best offer. They will be able to assess your chances of winning by looking at previous cases and use this knowledge to arrive at a sufficient figure that both sides can agree on. This can save all the expense and stress of going to court. Even if you win at court, you can be penalised if you did not accept an offer of settlement from the other side and the judgment at court turns out to be lower than the offer made beforehand.

- At court, a barrister is specifically trained in advocacy. They know the right things to say and the right time to say them. They are literally professional arguers. No matter how hard you try, the stress of going to court may mean that emotions take over in court and you end up shouting or crying in front of the judge. This will not help your case. Even though you may feel like you want to have your say, a barrister will take your words and choose what's relevant and, most importantly, what is going to sway the judge, without the emotion that will undoubtedly be attached when you say it. In a divorce, for example, emotions run extremely high and no one wants to see irrelevant dirty laundry aired across a courtroom. A barrister will know how to read the judge, possibly from having been in front of them many times before, and will therefore know how to run your case with the best chances of success. They will know what annoys or pleases that particular judge.

- In the end, the money you saved by not paying lawyers could easily be cancelled out by any penalties you are made to pay for not following procedure, or simply by not winning your case, not knowing how to present your evidence to show the court that you deserved to win. A decent lawyer is duty-bound to act in your best interests, using all their knowledge and experience to help you win your case. Going it alone can often be a false economy. In addition, you have safeguards in law against a lawyer who gives you bad advice. If you mess up, you have no one but yourself to blame.

- Don't forget to use the free services of places like the Citizens Advice Bureaux or local law centres, before you seek advice from solicitors or instead of talking to a solicitor. These places do incredible work.

- If you do decide to represent yourself, there is a lot of information available online. Websites such as www.help4lips. co.uk are good sources of help and advice. You will be allowed to have someone with you to help you in court by taking notes or giving you advice. These are called 'McKenzie friends'. They cannot, however, speak for you or interfere with proceedings.

SMALL CLAIMS: A HOW-TO GUIDE

THE SMALL CLAIMS COURT IN ENGLAND AND WALES

What kind of claims can I bring to the small claims court?

- If the financial value of the claim is less than £10,000.

- A claim for compensation for faulty goods and services.

- A claim for wages owed or money in lieu of notice.

- Disputes between landlords and tenants, e.g. rent arrears.

- In a personal injury case, if the claim for damages for pain, suffering or loss of amenity is less than £1,000.

- A claim by a tenant against a landlord where the tenant wants the landlord to carry out repairs or other works to the premises, if the cost of those repairs is less than £1,000.

- If you are within the time limits for your type of claim. For example, in a contract claim (like one for goods and services) you have six years from when the breach occurred.

If the claim is particularly complex, even if below the values stated above, the court can order that it be heard in another track, such as the multi-track or the fast track. If this is the case, seek legal advice. Ask your local CAB for help.

You do not need to be represented by a lawyer at the small claims court, though you can if you want to. It is designed to be informal and straightforward. There is a lot of guidance on the website www.gov.uk/make-court-claim-for-money/overview.

How to issue a claim in the small claims court

Before issuing a claim, you must, must, must try settling the claim first. Speak to the other party and try to sort things out. If that doesn't work, try one of the mediation services available. For example, there is a free telephone-based service offered through the Small Claims Mediation Service which you can try if both sides agree to it. If you don't try to settle first, the court may penalise you.

If that doesn't solve the issue, you need to proceed with making a small court claim. Go to the HM Courts and Tribunals section of www.justice.gov.uk and download the Claim Form (N1). If it's purely a money claim, you can start the claim online. If not, or if you do not want to do that, you should send or take the form to the court you wish to start the claim in, either the County Court Money Claims Centre for purely money claims, or otherwise your local county court.

On your Claim Form you need to include:
- Your details and the other side's details, and how much you are claiming.
- Any particulars of claim document. You can either include this on the space on the form, or you can attach it in a separate document. You can send this in with the Claim Form, or if you need extra time, you can send it within 14 days of sending the Claim Form.
- You may want to claim interest on the money. You must say how much. You can use the guidance notes attached to the Claim Form to help with this.
- You should include any relevant documents, e.g. a copy of the contract.

Take or send two copies of the Claim Form to the court. Remember to keep a copy for yourself. Include the court fee. This will vary depending on the kind of claim and how much it is worth. See www.justice.org.uk for details of fees. You might be able to get a fee remission – a reduction or waiver of the fees.

The court will stamp the Claim Form, and usually they will serve it on the defendant by first-class post. The defendant will be deemed to have received the Claim Form on the second business day after posting. You can serve it yourself if you ask the court office; they will give you the forms you need to include with the Claim Form.

The defendant will be asked if they:
- accept the claim
- wish to defend the claim
- want to acknowledge service and need more time to get back to you with further details (they have 14 days)

After the Claim Form has been served

- If the defendant accepts the claim, they can either pay you the money straight away or ask if you agree to them sending the money at a certain time or in instalments. If you accept this offer, you need to return a form to court requesting judgment on admission. If the defendant does not pay, you can take legal action to force them to do so. If you don't accept the offer, you must give your reasons and a court official will decide what is reasonable.

- If the defendant wants to defend the claim, they must return the Defence Form within 14 days of being deemed to have received your Claim Form. (Of, if they sent an acknowledgement of service, within 28 days). This will set out the reasons as to why they are defending the claim.

- If the defendant does not get back to you within the time allowed, you can apply to the court for a judgment in default. This means the defendant has to pay up.

- If the defendant does serve the Defence Form, both you and the defendant will be sent a directions questionnaire by the court. This will have questions about the case which will help the court decide whether your claim is appropriate for the small claims track, or another track. This must be returned by the date stated on the questionnaire.

- Then both parties will be sent a notice of allocation if the court thinks the case should be allocated to the small claims court. This notice will tell the parties what they have to do to prepare for the final hearing, which might include dates when documents need to be sent to court and to the other side. These instructions are called 'directions'. If you don't follow these directions, the case could be postponed and you could have to pay all the costs of the case.

- The notice of allocation might state the date, time and place of the hearing. If you cannot make it, you can request an alternative date if you have good reasons. You may need to pay a fee. You can request that the hearing go on in your absence, e.g. if you live far away and it would cost more than the value of the claim to get there. You must notify the court and the defendant no later than seven days before the hearing if this is the case.

- The notice of allocation may alternatively:
  - propose that the claim is dealt with without a hearing. If the parties do not object, the case will be decided from the documents that you and the defendant have sent in only. If the parties do not reply by the date given, the judge may treat the lack of reply as consent.
  - hold a preliminary hearing. This could happen if the claim requires special directions which the judge wants to explain to the parties personally, or where the judge feels that the claimant (or the defendant) has no real prospect of succeeding and wants to sort out the claim as soon as possible to save everyone time and expense, or if the papers do not show any reasonable grounds for bringing the claim. A preliminary hearing, therefore, could become a final hearing where the matter is decided once and for all.

- Make sure you prepare for the hearing, whether final or preliminary, carefully. Have all your evidence in order, and make sure you have everything you need to prove your case. Set things out in a way that makes it clear to you what you will be arguing. If you understand it and can present it clearly and efficiently, you will be in a much better position to get the court on your side. If possible, bring along the faulty product. Take photos of the shoddy service. You might need to prepare an expert report, e.g. with details of how your washing machine is faulty, or want to bring a witness along (you will need the permission of the court for these). Any expenses you have incurred should be evidenced with receipts.

The hearing

- This will be informal and strict rules of evidence do not apply (i.e. you will not be asked to swear on oath).

- It will usually be in public, though if the case warrants it, it might be in private.

- The judge can adopt any approach they feel appropriate. Don't expect it to be like what you see on TV.

- The judge can limit the amount of time given to evidence.

- You will be able to present your case and the other side will be able to respond. If you have prepared properly, you should be able to do this in a way that is understandable and persuasive. Do not get angry. Take your time. Be calm.

Don't worry if you are nervous, the judge will be accommodating. But they might not be if you start shouting.

- The judge will be more sympathetic if you can set out the lengths you have gone to in an attempt to settle the claim before coming to court.

- After hearing from both sides, the judge will give their judgment and they have to give reasons why they came to that conclusion. If you did not attend court, you will be sent a letter containing the judgment.

- If you win, you will get the court fees back, as well as what the judge has ordered. If you have evidence of your expenses, you should be able to claim those too.

- If you lose, you are unlikely to have to pay other costs, but you won't get your court fees back.

- You can appeal the decision if you are not happy, but only if there has been a mistake in law or if there was a serious irregularity in the proceedings. It probably would be best to seek advice from the CAB or a solicitor about what grounds you may have. Purely being unhappy with the decision won't be enough.

- Unless the court says otherwise, you will have 21 days from the date of the decision to appeal, by filing a notice of appeal with the court. You will have to pay an appeal fee, unless you get a fee remission.

What if the defendant still won't pay?

- You can go back to court to apply to get the money by way of an enforcement order.

- You will have to pay a fee for this, but you will likely get it back, along with the rest of your money.

- It would be wise to seek legal advice about enforcing the judgment and how best to go about it.

THE SMALL CLAIMS PROCEDURE IN SCOTLAND

What kind of claims can I bring to the sheriff (small claims) court?

- If the financial value of the claim is less than £3,000.

- A claim for payment of money.

- A claim for delivery or recovery of movable property.

- A claim for implementation of an obligation.

- Actions for recovery of possession of heritable property and personal injuries claims cannot be brought to the sheriff court. If the value is up to £5,000, then the summary cause procedure must be used, and above £5,000, the ordinary cause procedure. In these cases, you should seek advice from a solicitor.

You do not need to use a solicitor to use the small claims procedure, but you can if you wish. You can contact any of the organisations below for advice.

The small claims procedure is designed to be quick, cheap and easy to use. There is a lot of guidance available on the Scottish Courts and Tribunals website: www.scotcourts.gov.uk/taking-action/small-claims

Where can I get help?

There are many organisations which can help if you are considering beginning or defending a small claim.

- Scottish Association of Law Centres

- Citizens Advice Bureaux

- Consumer Advice centres

- Consumer Protection departments

- In-court adviser at Aberdeen, Airdrie, Dundee, Edinburgh, Hamilton and Kilmarnock Sheriff Courts

- Money Advice, Scotland

- Sheriff clerks' offices

- Trading Standards departments

HOW TO ISSUE A CLAIM IN THE SHERIFF COURT

Before issuing a claim, you must, must, must try settling the claim first. Speak to the other party and try to sort things out. Send a formal letter stating your complaint. If that doesn't work, try one of the mediation services available.

↓

If that doesn't solve the issue, you need to use the small claims procedure at the sheriff court. To raise a claim against an individual you will need to complete Form 1a and to raise a claim against a company or a voluntary association you will need to complete Form 1b. In both circumstances, you will also need to complete Form 1, which is the court copy of the summons. These forms are available from www.scotcourts.gov.uk/taking-action/small-claims or from your local sheriff clerk's office. You will also need to pay fees to the court. Ask the sheriff clerk what the fees will be for your particular case. You may be able to get a fee waiver.

↓

On Form 1a and Form1b, you need to include:
- Your details and the other side's details, and how much/ what you are claiming.
- In the statement of claim on page 2 of the form, you must give the defender fair notice of what the claim is about.
- The space on the form should normally be sufficient for you to complete the statement of claim. If not, you can add a separate sheet to the summons.
- You may want to claim interest on the money. You just say how much. You can use the guidance notes to help with this.

↓

Once you have completed the summons, you should go on to complete the defender's copy of the summons and take or send both to the sheriff clerk's office. A fee may be payable. The sheriff clerk will check that you have completed the forms correctly, complete section 6 of Form 1 and insert the summons number in the top right-hand corner.

↓

The defender needs to be served a copy of the summons. You aren't allowed to serve a copy on them yourself. The sheriff clerk will do it if you are an individual or a sole trader. Otherwise, you need to pay a solicitor or sheriff officer to do it for you.

↓

The defender can:
- do nothing
- admit the claim and settle the case
- admit the claim and make a written application about payment
- admit the claim and attend court to make an application about payment
- dispute the claim and attend court.

After the summons has been served

- The defender will be given a return date by which time they need to send a response, which was fixed by the sheriff clerk when you went to the court and lodged the summons.

- The defender responds by returning the appropriate pages of the copy summons to the court, outlining what they wish to do.

- It is your responsibility to check with the court immediately after the return date whether the defender has made a response.

- The defender may admit the claim and settle the case. They should make a payment to you or do what you have asked them to. If you are satisfied with this, you need to notify the sheriff clerk immediately and ask them to dismiss the case.

- The defender may admit the claim but make an application to the court to be allowed to pay the debt in instalments or in a lump sum within a specified period of time. The defender does this by making an application to the court for either a time to pay direction or a time order. Forms to apply for both of these applications are contained in the defender's copy summons. You will then have to decide whether you are prepared to accept it or not, and inform the court of your decision.

- The defender may respond to the summons by indicating that they admit the claim but wish to attend court to make an application about paying any sum of money due. The defender will indicate this by responding to that effect to the court on or before the return date.

- The defender may dispute the claim and wish to attend court. The defender will send a response to the court, indicating their position, before the hearing date.

- You must attend or be represented at court on the hearing date. If you fail to attend or be represented, your claim may be dismissed, and you may have to pay the defender's expenses.

- If the defender does not respond to the summons, you will have to let the court know what order you wish it to make. This should be done by lodging a written minute, using Form 11, which can be found on the Scottish Courts and Tribunals website. You must make your request at least two days (before the court closes, on a working day) before the date set for the hearing. You can request an order for the sum of money claimed, for something to be done (e.g. delivery of goods), or for the case to be continued.

The hearing

- The hearing date will have been set for 14 days after the return date.

- Make sure you prepare for the hearing carefully. Have all your evidence in order, and make sure you have everything you need to prove your case. Set things out in a way that makes it clear to you what you will be arguing. If you understand it and can present it clearly and efficiently, you will be in a much better position to get the court on your side.

- The hearing will be informal and in public.

- You will be able to present your case and the other side will be able to respond. If you have prepared properly, you should be able to do this in a way that is understandable and persuasive. Do not get angry. Take your time. Be calm. Don't worry if you are nervous, the sheriff will be accommodating. But they might not be if you start shouting.

- The sheriff will be more sympathetic if you can set out the lengths you have gone to in an attempt to settle the claim before coming to court.

- The sheriff might come to a decision at the end of the hearing or, alternatively, may need time to consider it. If further time is required, a decision will be issued in writing within 28 days of the hearing. The sheriff clerk will send a copy of the decision to the parties on receiving it from the sheriff.

- The sheriff will either:
  - Make a decree in favour of the pursuer (i.e. you've won!).
  - Make a decree of absolvitor in favour of the defender (a fancy way to say you have lost, and cannot apply again).
  - Dismiss the claim (you've lost but you can apply again).

- If you wish to appeal, you must lodge a note of appeal with the sheriff clerk within 14 days of the date of the sheriff's final decision, setting out the points of law upon which you wish to appeal. A fee is payable to the sheriff clerk when the appeal is registered.

What if the defender still won't pay?

- You can go back to court to apply to get the money by way of an enforcement order.

- You will have to pay a fee for this, but will likely get it back, along with the rest of your money.

- It would be wise to seek legal advice about enforcing the judgment and how best to go about it.

- Further information on enforcement procedures is contained in a leaflet called 'How to enforce your small claim decree'. A copy of this leaflet can be obtained from The Society of Messengers-at-Arms and Sheriff Officers,
11 Alva Street
Edinburgh EH2 4PH
or from one of the organisations listed above.

APPENDIX

USEFUL ADDRESSES

CUSTODY

Reunite International Child Abduction Centre
PO Box 7124
Leicester LE1 7XX
Tel: 0116 2556 234
www.reunite.org

Central Authority for England and Wales
The International Child Abduction and Contact Unit
Viceroy House
30–34 Kingsway
London WC2B 6EX
Tel: 020 3681 2608
Email: enquiries@offsol.gsi.gov.uk
Fax: 020 3681 2763
www.justice.gov.uk

Central Authority for Scotland
International and Human Rights Branch
St Andrew's House
Regent Road
Edinburgh EH1 3DG
Tel: 0131 244 4827 or 0131 244 4826
www.gov.scot

TRADESMEN

Electricians

NICEIC Certification Services – maintains a register of qualified and competent electricians www.niceic.com

British Standards Institution (BSI) – offers a Kitemark scheme for electrical installers www.kitemark.com

Electrical Competent Person Scheme – a Competent Person Scheme for electricians www.electricalcompetentperson.co.uk

National Association of Professional Inspectors and Testers (NAPIT) – also holds a Competent Person Scheme register of electricians www.napit.org.uk

Gas fitters

Gas Safe Register
PO Box 6804
Basingstoke
RG24 4NB
Tel: 0800 408 5500 www.gassaferegister.co.uk

EMPLOYMENT

The Acas helpline is 0300 123 1100. The helpline is open 8am–8pm Monday to Friday and 9am–1pm on Saturdays. Their website is www.acas.org.uk

GENERAL LEGAL ADVICE

Citizens Advice Bureaux are a great place to start. Go online to find your local branch. Their website also contains lots of useful advice guides: www.citizensadvice.org.uk

Other places you can seek help include the Bar Pro Bono Unit, the Free Representation Unit (FRU), LawWorks or a local Law Centre. All of their details will be online, and their websites will set out what help they can give.

ACKNOWLEDGEMENTS

To the sublime Holly Baxter who made writing this utterly joyful. Bethany Condron who spared me inordinate stress (as ever). The vision and visionary that is Helen Warner without whom none of this would have happened. The peculiar genius of Tom Mclennan along with Kate Broadhurst and the dazzling talents of the entire *Judge Rinder* team at ITV Studios. To Joanne and Sam Koukis-Robinson who provided me with a home (and so much more besides). Jeremy and Louisa Brier for their limitless brilliance and humour. My OJ and her heavenly kitchen. Grant Michaels who promises he has read the book. Benedict Cumberbatch and Sophie Hunter for giving me the kit I needed to help finish the book. Ben Dunn and Ajda Vucicevic who make one believe that anything is possible (except for making striped jumpers work). To my family – all of you; you are the reason I have been able to do what I love. And lastly to Uncle Mark, who would have found this amusing.